Editor
Kathy Humrichouse

Editorial Project Manager
Paul Gardner

Editor in Chief
Sharon Coan, M.S. Ed.

Art Coordinator
Denice Adorno

Creative Director
Elayne Roberts

Imaging
Alfred Lau
James Edward Grace

Product Manager
Phil Garcia

Acknowledgments:
Internet Explorer software is ©1983–2000 Microsoft Corporation. All Rights Reserved. *Internet Explorer* is a registered trademark of Microsoft Corporation.

Publishers:
Rachelle Cracchiolo, M.S. Ed.
Mary Dupuy Smith, M.S. Ed.

Microsoft®
Internet Explorer
for
Terrified Teachers

Author:

Debi Hooper

Teacher Created Materials, Inc.
6421 Industry Way
Westminster, CA 92683
www.teachercreated.com

©2000 Teacher Created Materials, Inc.
Made in U.S.A.
ISBN-1-57690-444-X

Table of Contents

Table of Contents *(cont.)*

Introduction

You have been hearing about the Net, e-mail, newsgroups, graphics, multimedia, and teleconferencing. Now that you have access to the Internet and this software package, where do you start? Welcome to Microsoft's *Internet Explorer*, one of the leading Internet access suites. With this software package, you will be able to do all of those things and more.

This book will lead you through all of the components of the *Internet Explorer* software suite and explain how you can use the components within your classroom. There will be step-by-step instructions for setting up your *Internet Explorer* utilities and for accessing resources on the Internet to use with your curriculum.

The *Internet Explorer* suite has four components that are integrated, or work together, to provide you with access to the Internet's resources.

Internet Explorer—This component is one you will use most often. It is your web browser, or the software you will use to access Web pages on the World Wide Web.

Outlook Express—This is your e-mail (or electronic mail) and newsgroup software component. You will use it to send and receive messages with other Internet users. By setting up newsgroups, you will be able to access messages from groups of other Internet users about a variety of subjects. There are hundreds of newsgroups about special topics and software packages.

NetMeeting—With this utility, you can conference with other teachers and classes around the world. If you have a camera and microphone attached to your computer, you can see and talk with them as well.

FrontPage Express—You can use this component to help you design and publish your own Web pages. It is a Hypertext Markup Language, or HTML, editor. You can create your pages "from scratch" or use the Wizards.

Using This Book

This book will be divided into sections about each of the components of *Internet Explorer*. Within each section, you will read directions for setting up and using the component, and there will be suggestions for integrating its use into your curriculum.

As you read this book, these graphics will mark items of interest, to help you or provide you with reminders.

 Note:—There will be notes throughout the book, which will be reminders or will direct you to instructions in other parts of the book.

 Web page—You will be advised to key in different URLs or Universal Resource Locators (Web page addresses).

 Help—This icon will direct you to more information about a topic or help with instructions throughout the book.

The following font styles will be used throughout the book.

Bold Italic Words in bold italic will show you which menu items you should click as you follow directions.

Italics Items in italic are words you will be asked to key in.

 Note: The instructions and graphics in this book will apply to *Internet Explorer* for *Windows 95*. The instructions should be the same or similar for Macintosh users.

Using the Internet

What is the Internet? If your school has a network, then you have already experienced something similar to the Internet. A network is simply a group of computers connected to each other by cables. This is done so that they can all access one main computer (called a file server) and share files. That network is called a LAN or Local Area Network.

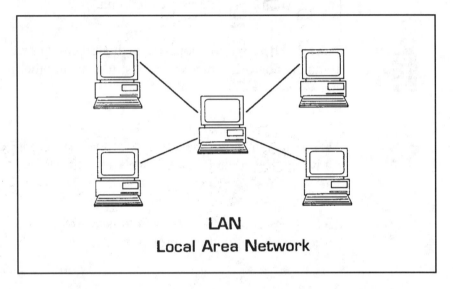

LAN
Local Area Network

If your building's network is also connected to other buildings in your school district, then you have a WAN or Wide Area Network.

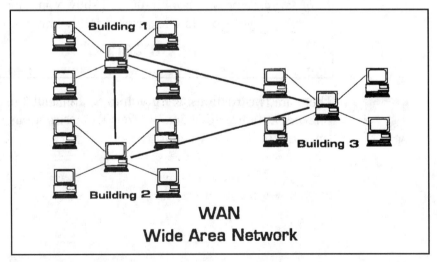

WAN
Wide Area Network

This is exactly what the Internet is. It is a large network of computers and file servers in different buildings, cities, states, and countries. The cables that connect these computers range from fiber optic cables to twisted copper cables to telephone lines.

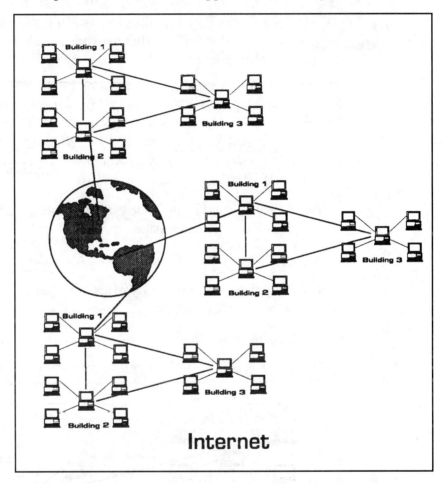

Internet

There are two basic ways for you to be connected to the Internet. The first way is by dialing an Internet Service Provider or ISP. To do this, you must have a modem in your computer and an account with a provider. The other way is to be wired to the Internet through your school's network. In either instance, your access to the Internet through *Internet Explorer*'s software will be the same.

About *Internet Explorer*

Microsoft was formed in 1975, soon after the MITS Altair kit computer was released and promoted the programming language, BASIC (Beginners All-purpose Symbolic Instruction Code) for computers. Paul Allen and Bill Gates, who then created Microsoft as a business that would build software, developed BASIC.

With the release of graphical information on the World Wide Web, software developers needed to create browser software so computer users could access this information. NCSA Mosaic was the first graphical web browser. In 1995, Microsoft released its first version of *Internet Explorer*, which was developed for the *Windows 95* operating system.

Internet Explorer and its upgrades are available for download from the *Internet Explorer* home page:

http://www.microsoft.com/windows/ie/default.htm

The starting page, or home page, when you start using *Internet Explorer* is the **MSN** home page:

http://home.microsoft.com/

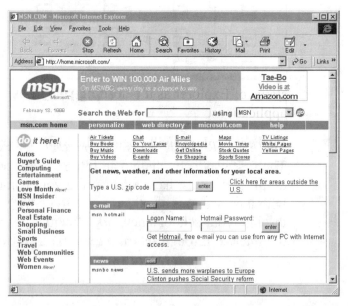

Starting Out

The component of this software you will use most is *Internet Explorer*. *Internet Explorer* is your World Wide Web browser. This is the software that will connect you to Web pages around the world. You will be able to keep bookmarks of your favorite Web sites, download files, and view graphics and multimedia.

 To start *Internet Explorer*, double-click the *Internet Explorer* icon on your desktop or in the *Internet Explorer* folder.

As the program starts, you will see this splash screen showing the status of Explorer as it is loading your bookmarks and plug-in applications.

Internet Explorer will open to the MSN (Microsoft Network) home page where you will be able to search for information, check your MSN Hotmail, and locate information from several basic groupings of topics.

Internet Explorer **Window**

The following elements are contained in the *Internet Explorer* window.

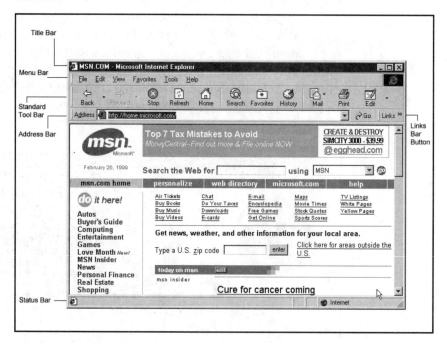

Title Bar—This bar shows the name of the Web page you are currently viewing.

Menu Bar—Like other programs, this bar appears at the top of the window and contains menus from which instructions for the program can be chosen.

Standard Tool Bar—This toolbar provides you with buttons to make your browsing easier. You will be able to click to go back to a previous page, go to the next page, refresh pages, stop loading pages, etc.

Address Bar—This shows you the current Web address (or URL) of the Web page you are viewing.

Status Bar—This bar shows the current loading status of a Web page. It will display what percentage of the page has finished downloading and any attached graphics, sound, or multimedia files that are loaded. It will also display the address, or URL, of any hyper-link you move your mouse across while viewing a Web page.

Links Bar Button—This button opens the Links Bar which contains links that you can click to go to a specific Web page quickly. You will find several pre-set links, but you can customize this bar with your own favorite links also.

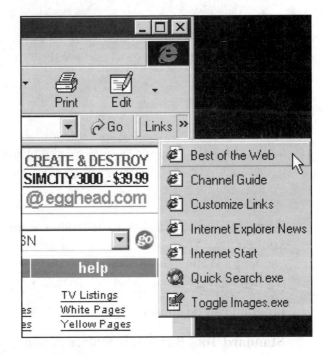

Standard Tool Bar

Take a closer look at the button options on *Internet Explorer's* Standard Tool Bar.

As you are browsing through Web pages, you will be able to click the **Back** button to return to previously viewed pages.

After viewing previous pages, you can click the **Forward** button to move forward in the series of viewed pages.

If you need to stop a Web page from loading, you can click the **Stop** button. There will be times when the connection between you and a Web page may be slow. Instead of waiting for a Web page to load, you can simply click this button and then go to a different Web page.

You can click the **Refresh** button to reload the current Web page if your transfer was interrupted for some reason.

You can click the *Home* button to return to whichever Web page you have designated as your home page. The default setting that was installed with the software returns you to the **MSN** home page.

When you click the *Search* button, your *Internet Explorer* window will divide into frames, and you will have several options appear in the **Search Explorer** bar in the left-hand frame.

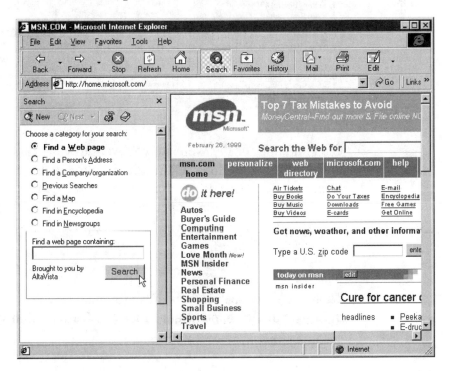

This will allow you to search for Web pages, maps, encyclopedia entries, newsgroups, etc.

This Web page search accesses **AltaVista's** database of Web sites.

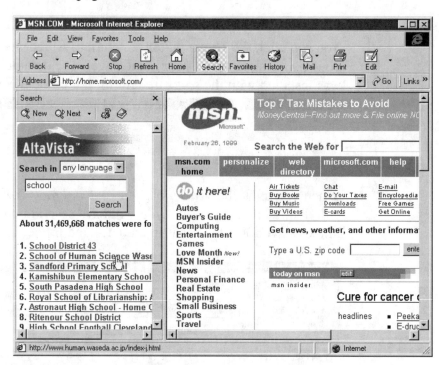

Click the link for the Web site you want to view, and it will appear in the right-hand frame. Once you have found a Web page you want to see in more detail, you can close the Search Explorer bar by clicking the X in the upper right-hand corner of that frame.

There are other search Web sites available, as well. They will be discussed in the chapter **Searching For Information** (page 171).

The **Favorites** button displays the **Favorites Explorer** bar in the left-hand frame of the *Internet Explorer* window.

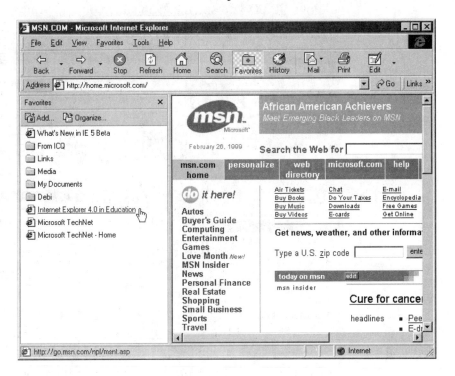

This allows you to access your favorite Web sites quickly by simply clicking the links in your list.

To close the **Favorites Explorer** bar, click the **X** in the upper right-hand corner of the frame.

When you click the *History* button, the **History Explorer** bar will
be displayed in the left-hand frame of your *Internet Explorer*
window. It lets you see the Web sites you and your students have
recently visited.

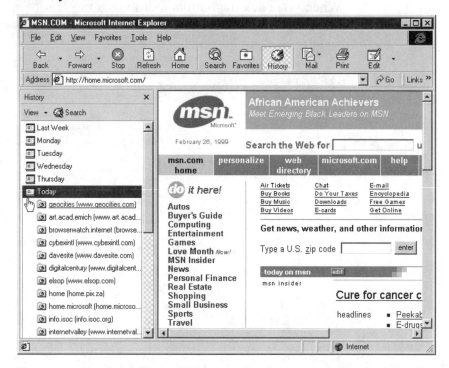

To open one of the files, click the calendar icon next to it. The list
of Web sites that were visited that day will appear in the **History
Explorer** bar. To re-visit one of the Web sites, click that link in
the list.

To close the **History Explorer** bar, click the X in the upper right-
hand corner of the frame.

The ***Mail*** button opens Microsoft *Outlook Express*. This component is for sending and receiving mail and reading newsgroups.

When you click the button, a drop-down menu will appear. Select the activity you want to perform and click its name in the list. You will also be able to send links to Web sites or send actual Web pages to people on your e-mail list.

By clicking the ***Print*** button, you can easily print the Web page you are currently viewing.

When you click the ***Edit*** button, you will be able to edit a Web page in an HTML editor. *FrontPage Express* is available for free download, or you can access the full version if you have it installed on your computer. (Not available for the Macintosh)

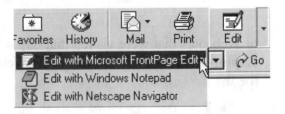

Select your choice from the drop-down menu and click to open that editing program.

Menu Bar

The menu bar on the *Internet Explorer* components gives you options for printing and viewing Web pages. You will use menu selections to insert your e-mail and newsgroup settings and to set other preferences. This will be an overview of the menu bar selections. Many of the menu selections will be the same in each of the *Internet Explorer* components.

By clicking each of the words on the menu bar, you will see a menu of additional choices drop down.

File Menu

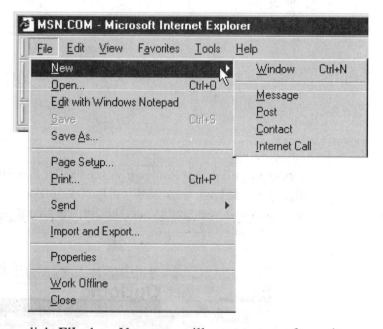

If you click *File* then *New*, you will see a menu of new items you can open on your screen. The first item is *Window*, which will open another *Internet Explorer* window. If you are viewing a Web page and want to go to another Web page without losing your place on the first page, you can choose to open another *Internet Explorer* window.

If you click *File*, then *New*, then *Message*, you will open the e-mail message window with a blank message screen available for you to write an e-mail. Macintosh users open *Outlook Express* by clicking the *Mail* button.

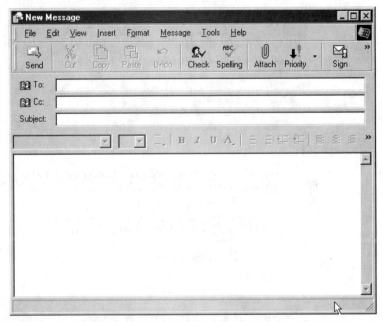

Choosing *File*, then *New*, then *Post* will open *Outlook Express* so that you can post a message to a newsgroup.

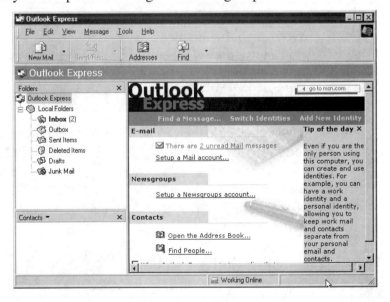

The *File*, then *New*, then *Contact* choice will allow you to quickly access contacts in your e-mail address book. You can then select from your list of names and e-mail addresses to send someone a message.

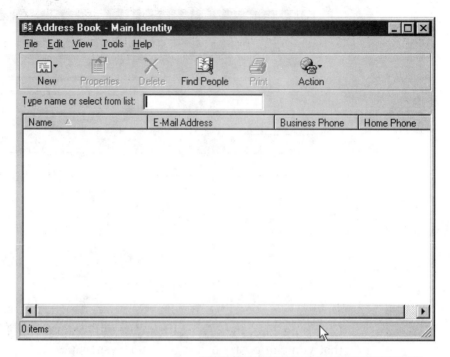

If you have Web pages saved on your computer, you can use the *File* then *Open* selections to open and view that Web page in your *Internet Explorer* window.

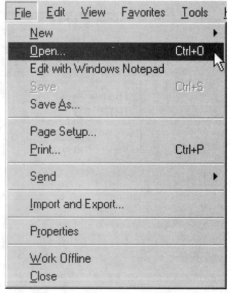

You will see this dialog box. You can either key in the filename of the Web page or click the **Browse** button to browse through the folders and files on your computer.

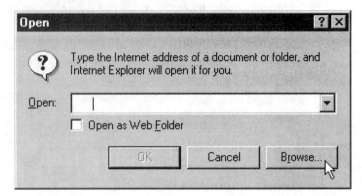

If you click the **Browse** button, you will get this dialog box where you can browse through the files on your computer and select the file you want to open.

Once you have selected the file you want to open, click the **Open** button from this dialog box and then click the **OK** button in the next dialog box.

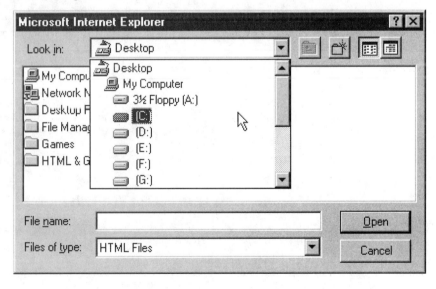

If you are viewing a Web page that you want to edit, you can select *File*, then *Edit with Microsoft FrontPage Editor* and you will open that Web page in the HTML editing program you have chosen in your options.

Note: Options will be explained in another section of this book.

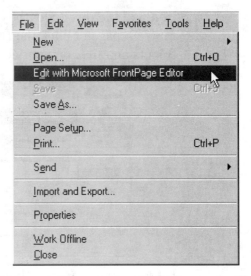

If you have *FrontPage Express* or *FrontPage*, the Web page will be opened in that HTML editor.

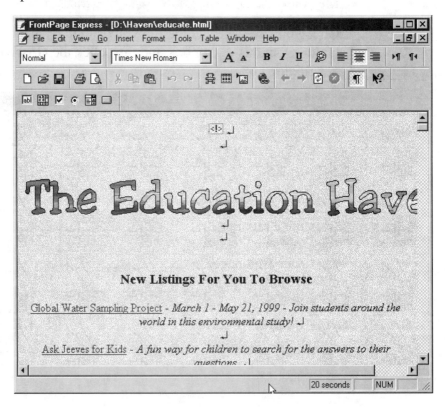

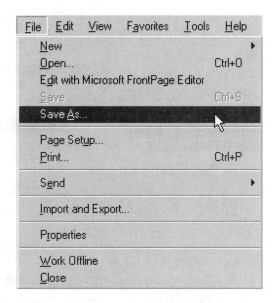

If you find a Web page online that you want to keep on your computer for reference, you can use the *Save As* command.

You will see the *Save Web Page* dialog box. You can then select the folder in which you would like to save the Web page.

You can choose to save the file as complete (with graphics) or as HTML only (without graphics).

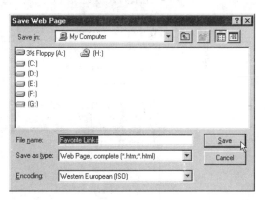

Note: It is a good idea to create a separate folder in which you will save your Web pages to easily find them later.

Quite often, you will want to print a hard copy of a Web page so that you can read it later or use it in your classroom. By clicking *File* then *Page Setup*, you can select several printing options. The *Page Setup* dialog box will be different for each printer, but the options will be similar.

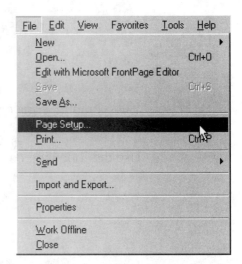

You can select different page margins and add or delete Header and Footer information.

The default, or normal print setup, includes the document title and URL as well as page numbers and the date printed.

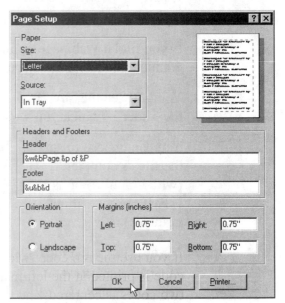

This is important information to have if you want to remember where and when you found the information. The document title and URL are also important when citing these pages as references.

If you need to edit the Header or Footer, codes will be needed to print additional information. Header and Footer cannot be edited using a Macintosh version.

The special codes find information from the Web page or from your computer. Each code is preceded by an ampersand (&) and is followed by a letter code.

Use the following codes to edit the Header or Footer

Code:	Information:
&w	The document title
&u	The Web page address or URL
&d	The current date from your computer's settings
&D	The current date in long format
&t	The current time from your computer's settings
&T	The current time in 24-hour format
&p	The page number
&P	The total number of pages
&&	Prints a single ampersand
&b	Specifies location of information

If you use the &b one time, the information to the left of the code is printed at the left margin, and the information to the right of the code is printed at the right margin.

If you use the &b code twice, the information to the left of the code is printed at the left margin, the information in between the two codes is centered, and the information to the right of the code is printed at the right margin.

You can also include text in the Header and Footer. Simply key in the text you want to appear. For example, Page &p would print as Page 1 or the applicable page number.

In order to print a Web page, click *File*, then *Print*.

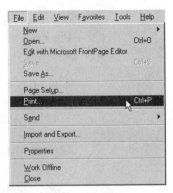

The *Print* dialog box will appear, and you will be able to select the printing options you want, such as which pages to print and how many copies you want of each page.

Note: Be sure the proper printer is selected before printing. If you will be using the Web page in the classroom, you may want to print it on transparency film. Be sure to select the *Properties* options button, and then choose *Best* quality for the printing option and *Transparency Film* as the paper option.

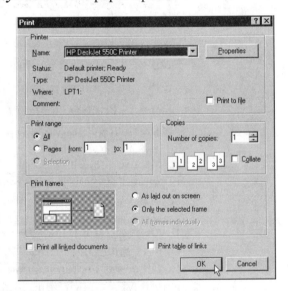

If you are viewing a Web page with frames, you can select whether to print the document as it appears on the screen or to print selected frames.

You can also print a table of the Web pages linked from the Web page you are viewing.

You can choose to print all of the Web pages linked from the Web page you are viewing, but be careful if you select this option. There may be hundreds of pages of linked Web sites.

Note: Be sure to advise your students not to select this option but to print only the pages they are actually viewing.

If you are viewing a Web page and would like to share it with someone else, you can click *File*, then *Send*. You will be given several options of how you can make note of the Web page.

By choosing *File*, *Send*, *Page By E-mail*, you can send the actual HTML file to someone via e-mail.

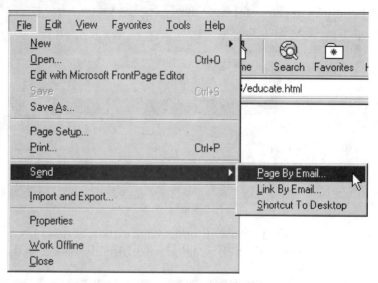

This choice will open your e-mail and include the Web page ready for you to send.

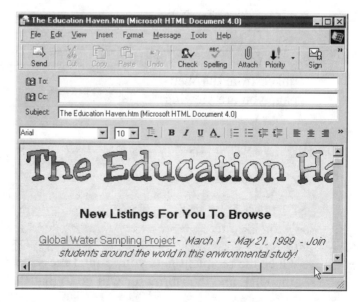

By selecting *File*, *Send*, *Link By E-mail*, you can send someone the URL of the Web page you are viewing.

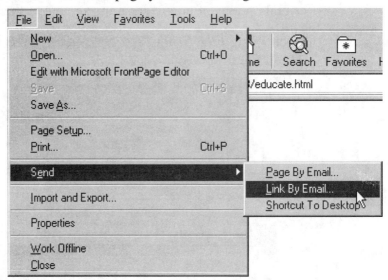

This option will open your e-mail and set up a message to be sent with the Web page address already added to the message.

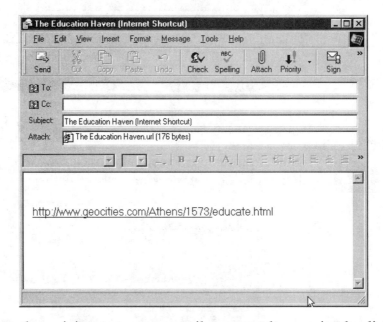

Once the recipient gets your e-mail message, he can simply click the URL and their browser will go to that Web page.

If you want to create a quick reminder so you can easily find the Web page again, you can have *Internet Explorer* set up a shortcut icon on your computer's desktop.

Click *File*, *Send*, *Shortcut To Desktop*. This will create an icon on your desktop area.

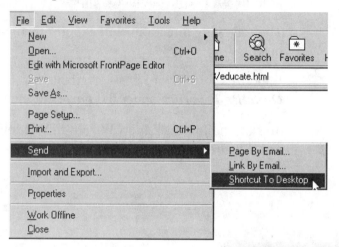

By having the shortcut, or icon, on your desktop, you can instruct students to use those specific Web pages in an activity for a specific lesson.

They can double-click the icon, and *Internet Explorer* will open and go directly to that Web page.

Note: You can create several shortcuts to Web pages and put them in a folder on your desktop organizing them by lesson or class.

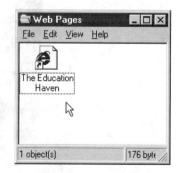

If you have Internet access at home and at school, you save and share a file containing your favorite Web sites. This is especially important if you have researched a list of Web sites that you want your students to visit in order to complete a lesson plan. You can organize your favorite sites into a folder and then save that folder as a file for use on another computer.

The following directions will export this file to a file on another disk.

Import/Export Wizard is not available for the Macintosh. Use *Organize Favorites* under the *Favorites* menu.

To start the Import/Export Wizard in Windows, click *File*, *Import and Export*.

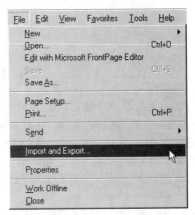

You will see this opening screen. Click the *Next* button to continue through the export process.

To save favorite Web sites to a file, select ***Export Favorites***. Click the ***Next*** button to continue.

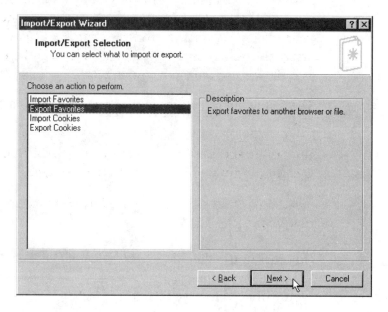

If you have organized your Favorites into folders, you can save your entire list of Favorites or you can choose just to save one folder. You can also save groups of Favorites into separate files. Select the correct folder and click the ***Next*** button.

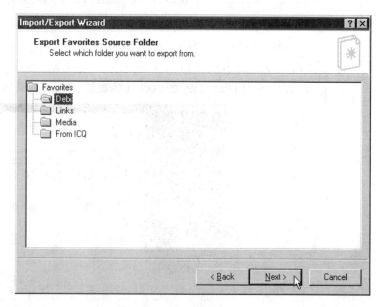

Select *Export to a File or Address*. Click the *Browse* button to choose where you want to save the file.

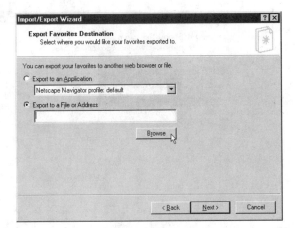

In order to use this file on another computer, you will need to save it to a disk in the A: drive.

Select the A: drive and click the *Save* button.

The filename *A:\bookmark.htm* will appear in the Export window. Click the *Next* button to continue.

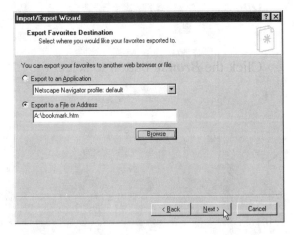

If you are still certain that you want to save this file, click the *Finish* button. The file will then be saved to the disk in the A: drive.

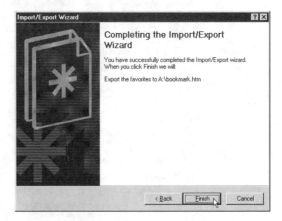

You will see this dialog box if the file was successfully saved to the diskette.

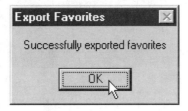

To view the file on this or another computer, select *File*, *Open*.

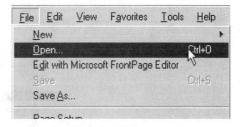

Click the *Browse* button to select the file from the diskette.

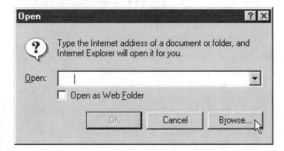

Select the file from the diskette in the A: drive and click the ***Open*** button.

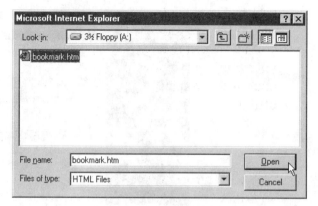

Click the ***OK*** button to open the file in *Internet Explorer*.

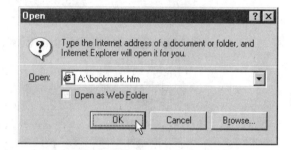

The file will open as an HTML file with hypertext links that you can click to go to the Web sites.

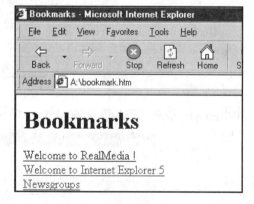

 Note: Once you become familiar with editing Web pages, you can edit this page and include lesson instructions for your students to complete while using your list of Web sites.

If you want to work on Web pages while you are offline, you can click *File*, *Work Offline*. This will allow you to keep your browser window open while you are offline.

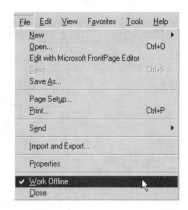

Note: If you are working with an offline browser program, such as *Web Buddy*, you can read the downloaded Web pages in your *Internet Explorer* window while offline. You can also use this option at school if you do not have online access from your classroom computer.

Once you select to work offline, you will be able to view any saved Web pages until you click *File*, *Work Offline* again. As you are browsing downloaded Web pages, *Internet Explorer* will advise you when you attempt to access a Web page you have not downloaded. It will ask if you want to go online or remain offline.

When you are finished working offline, be sure to click *File*, *Work Offline* to remove the checkmark. You will then be able to view online Web pages.

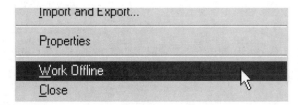

To close *Internet Explorer* and exit the program, click **File**, **Close**. This will close the *Internet Explorer* window while leaving any other program windows open.

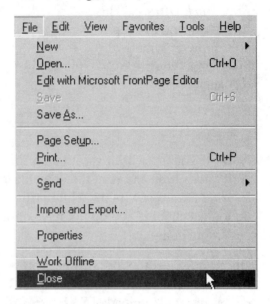

You can also close *Internet Explorer* by clicking the **X** button in the upper right-hand corner of the window.

Edit Menu

The *Edit* menu has many options for you to utilize. *Cut*, *Copy*, and *Paste* work in the same way as those features in a word processing program. You can copy sections of text and paste them into documents.

The *Find (on this page)* option allows you to search a Web page for specific text.

Click *Edit*.

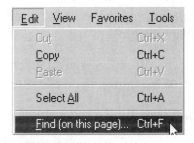

Click *Find (on this page)*.

The *Find* dialog box will appear. Key in the text you wish to find in the document. Once you have keyed text into the blank, the *Find Next* button will become active.

Click the *Find Next* button to perform the search.

If the text appears on the Web page, *Internet Explorer* will scroll down to that line and the text will be highlighted.

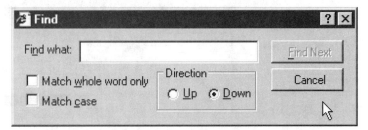

View Menu

The *View* menu allows you to pick what you want to see in your *Internet Explorer* window.

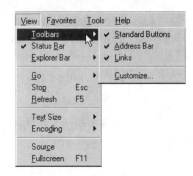

Click *View*.

Click *Toolbars*.

Note: As you and your students learn to use the various *Internet Explorer* components, it is recommended that you leave all of the toolbars visible.

You can customize your Standard Toolbar by adding or removing some of the buttons you use often or do not use often enough.

Click *View*, *Toolbars*, *Customize*.

You will use this dialog box to add and remove buttons. You can also choose to show text labels on your toolbar buttons.

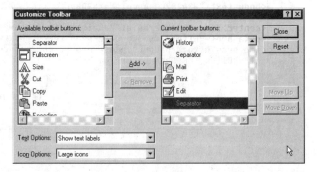

To customize toolbars for Macintosh users, choose *Preferences* under the *Edit* menu.

In order to see what the HTML coding for a Web page looks like, choose the *Source* option.

Click *View*.

Click *Source*.

A Notepad window will open. The coding for the current web page (or frame within a Web page) will appear.

Looking at the source code for interesting Web pages will give you and your students ideas about how to create your own pages.

Favorites Menu

Favorites are URLs or Web site addresses that you want to keep organized for easy and quick retrieval. You could write down the address of every one of your favorite Web sites, but this utility will do the work for you much more efficiently.

The *Favorites* button on the Toolbar shows you a list of your favorite Web sites in the left-hand portion of your *Internet Explorer* window. The Favorites menu gives you the ability to manipulate that list.

Once you have found a Web site that you want to mark as a favorite, click *Favorites*.

Then click *Add to Favorites*.

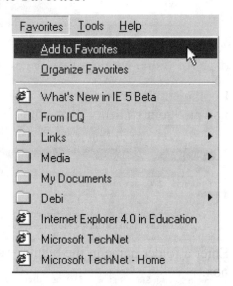

The title of the Web page will appear in the *Name* blank, and you can add this to your list of favorite sites by clicking the *OK* button.

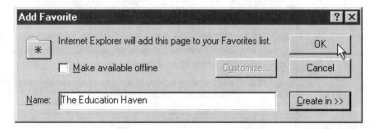

By clicking the ***Create in*** button, you add options for organizing your favorites.

You can select a folder in which to save the new listing.

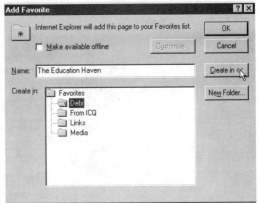

Click the ***OK*** button, and the favorite will then be listed in that folder.

You can create new folders by clicking the ***New Folder*** button.

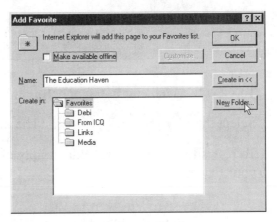

Enter a folder name in the blank on the **Create New Folder** dialog box.

Click the ***OK*** button and *Internet Explorer* will create the folder in your Favorites list.

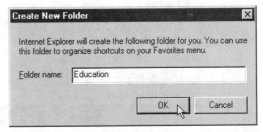

Once you have created the new folder, click to select it.

Then click the *OK* button to place the favorites listing in that folder.

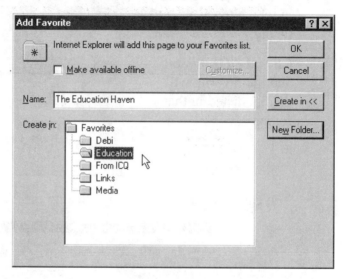

To view the Web site in the new folder, click ***Favorites***.

Select the new folder, *Education*. The new listing is shown there.

To re-visit that site, you would simply click the Web site name in your Favorites list.

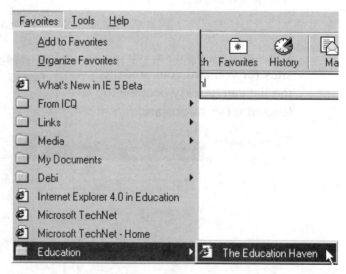

Another good reason to create custom folders within your Favorites list is to use the folders when exporting your favorites into an HTML file.

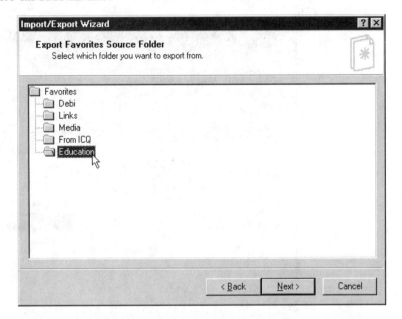

When you use the Export Wizard, you do not have to export your entire Favorites list. You can select a single folder of Favorites to be exported.

Another reason for creating custom folders is to keep your Favorites list organized. Once you start finding good reference sites for you and your students, the list can quickly become too long to serve its purpose.

To manage your favorites, click *Favorites*, *Organize Favorites*.

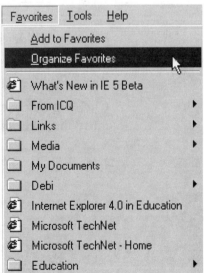

You can use the Organize Favorites dialog box to create new folders, rename favorites or folders, and delete references you no longer need. You can also move listings of favorites into new folders.

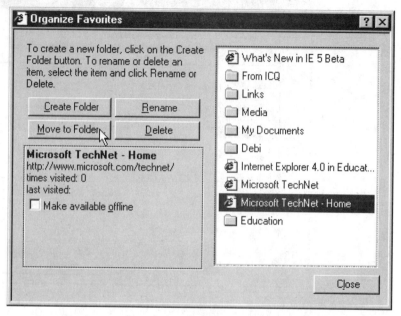

To move a favorite, click the ***Move to Folder*** button.

Select the folder into which you want to move the favorite.

Click the ***OK*** button to move the favorite listing.

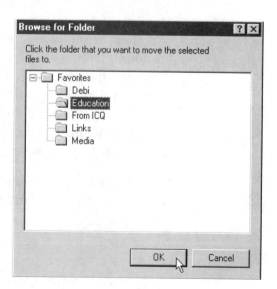

By clicking the folder, you can open it and see what favorites are listed in it. You should see the favorite that you just moved.

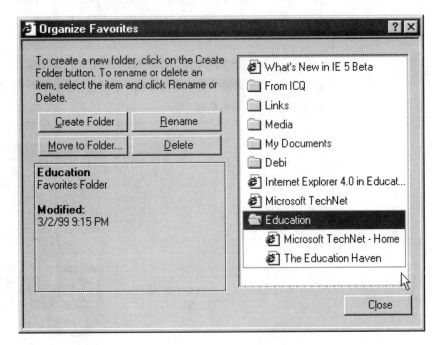

Click the **Close** button when you have finished organizing your Favorites list.

You will also see the new listing when you view your Favorites list by clicking **Favorites**, **Education**.

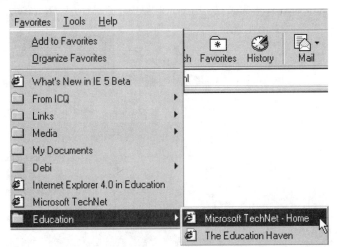

Tools Menu

The Tools Menu allows you to quickly access your e-mail and newsgroups and to set up some program options.

To check your e-mail, you can use the button on the Standard Button Bar or you can use the Tools Menu options. The Tools Menu is not available on the Macintosh. Use the *Mail* icon for accessing *Outlook Express*.

Click *Tools*.

Click *Mail & News*.

Click *Read Mail*.

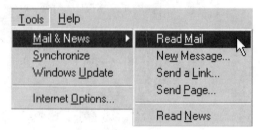

This will open Microsoft *Outlook Express*, and you will be able to access your incoming e-mail.

You will see the splash screen for *Outlook Express* as it opens.

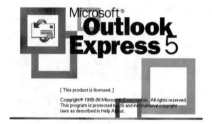

The *Outlook Express* window will be separate from the *Internet Explorer* window. You can check and send e-mail, then close that program without affecting your *Internet Explorer* task.

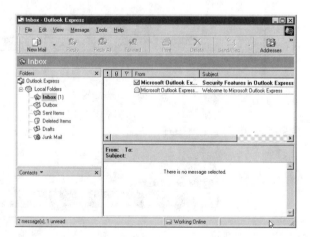

You can quickly send an e-mail message by using the *New Message* option.

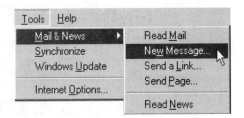

Click *Tools*, *Mail & News*, *New Message*.

The message window will appear. You can enter the e-mail address and Subject line, then write and send your e-mail message.

The *Send a Link* and *Send Page* selections work just as the options in the File Menu. Through these selections, you are able to send a URL or a complete Web page to your e-mail recipient.

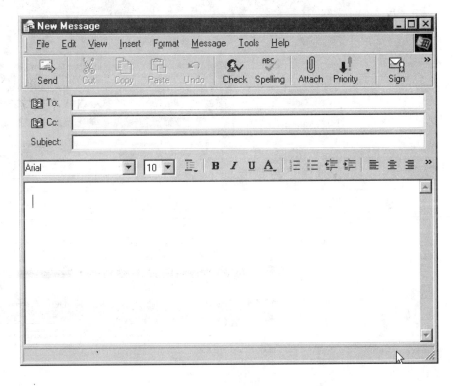

To read your newsgroups, select ***Tools***, ***Mail & News***, ***Read News***.

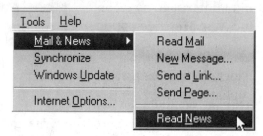

This will open *Outlook Express* to your newsgroup listing. You can then read and send messages.

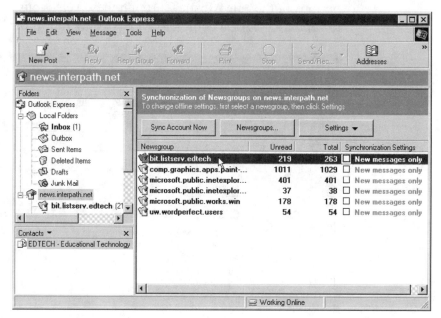

 Note: Setting up and using newsgroups will be explained in the *Outlook Express* section of this book.

If you have set some of your
Favorites to be available when you
are offline, then you need to update
them periodically.

Select ***Tools***, then ***Synchronize*** to
update the files.

You will be given the option of synchronizing any or all of the
Web pages you have marked.

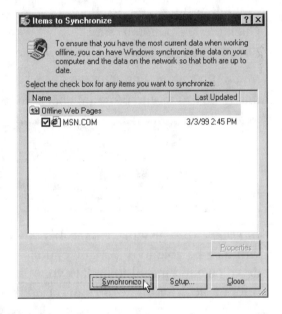

The ***Synchronizing*** dialog box will advise you of the progress of
your update. You can also stop the process, if you need to, by
clicking the ***Stop*** button.

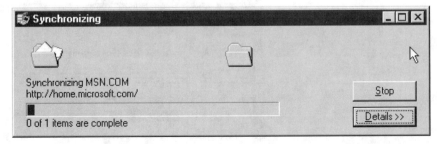

To maintain your *Internet Explorer* and make sure you have the latest additional program options, you should update it periodically.

Select *Tools*, *Windows Update*.

The first time you access *Windows Update*, you will see this dialog box. The *Windows Update* utility must read your hard drive and find out what program utilities are installed. Click the *Yes* button to start this process.

You will also need to click the *Yes* button on the *Windows Update* dialog box to let the program check your hard drive.

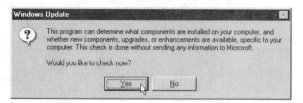

Internet Explorer will load the *Windows Update* Web page. You will then be able to select any options or utilities you want to download and install to update your program. Macintosh users refer to the *Microsoft* Web site for updates.

You will use the ***Internet Options*** choice to set up how you want *Internet Explorer* to function.

Select ***Tools***, ***Internet Options***.

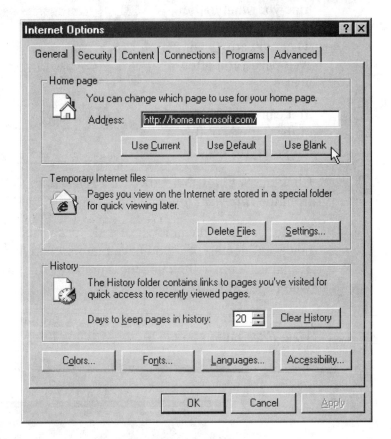

You can set the page you will view when *Internet Explorer* opens. If you are able to write your own Web page, you may want to designate that page on your computer as you opening page. It is much faster for *Internet Explorer* to open with a page on the local computer than to have to look online for a Web page.

You can also choose to have it open with a blank page if your Internet connection is slow. This will also allow you to use *Internet Explorer* easily even when you are not online.

Internet Explorer uses a temporary folder in which to keep Web page files and associated graphics handy for the next time you want to view them. This helps when you are viewing Web pages you often visit.

You can change some of the settings of this temporary folder.

Click the *Settings* (Windows) or *Preferences* (Macintosh) button from the *Internet Options* dialog page.

Do not decrease the amount of disk space used. You can, however, increase it if you have memory and hard drive space available. This will reduce the amount of time it takes for those Web pages to load.

If you want to view those Web pages or graphics files, click the *View Files* button on the *Settings* dialog box.

Double-click any of the Web pages or files to view them.

Note: This is a good way to double-check where your students have been browsing. The URL of visited Web pages is listed in this content file.

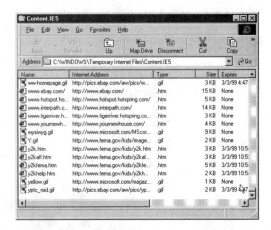

If you are having difficulty loading Web pages, you may want to clear the contents of the temporary folder.

To do this, click the *Delete Files* button.

This will remove any Web pages or graphics that have been stored in that folder.

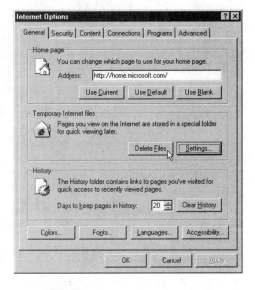

You will see this confirmation box when you choose to delete the files. To proceed, simply click the *OK* button. To delete all stored content for viewing Web pages offline, click to make a checkmark in that box.

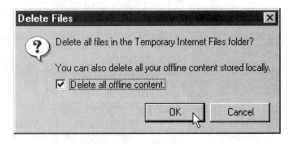

The History folder shows what Web sites you and your students have recently visited. Here you can set a specific number of days after which those history locations are deleted from the file. You can also click the *Clear History* button to delete those URLs from the list.

Note: If the computer is being used often and many pages are being visited, you may want to reduce the number of days the pages stay in the history. This will reduce the size of the file on your hard drive.

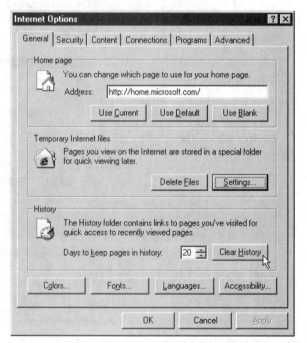

You will see a dialog box to confirm deletion of the items in the History folder.

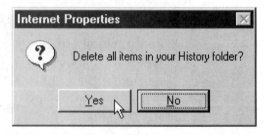

Click the *Yes* button to clear the contents.

Note: Remember that you can view the History file by clicking the *History* button on the Standard Tool Bar.

Click the ***Colors*** button to make changes in the appearance of your *Internet Explorer* window.

This may be helpful if you have students with vision problems who are having difficulty reading Web pages with colors which are not distinct.

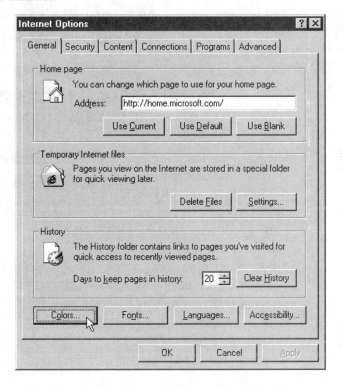

With this dialog box, you can easily choose to set your own colors for text, background, visited and unvisited links.

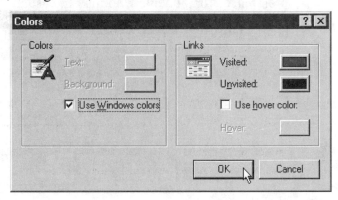

Click *Fonts* to change the appearance of your *Internet Explorer* fonts. If you have younger students who are having difficulty reading a particular font type, you can change that here.

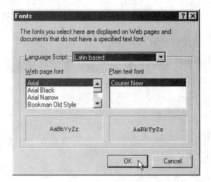

Click *Languages* to change the language option. You probably have only one language loaded into your *Internet Explorer* program. If, however, you have more than one and you find that your *Internet Explorer*

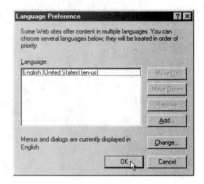

components are now speaking a different language or gibberish to you, you can come here to reset the language setting.

Click the *Accessibility* button to set your *Internet Explorer* window so that it ignores Web page settings and keeps your preferences for students who may be visually impaired.

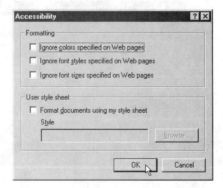

Click the *Security* tab to set those options.

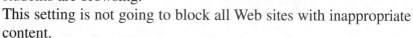

You may have a security setting requirement in your school's Acceptable Use Policy. If not, you may decide to use this setting to help filter out web sites with harmful content.

Note: You must also monitor where your students are browsing. This setting is not going to block all Web sites with inappropriate content.

Where you may want the Internet setting to be a High security level, you might set your Local Intranet to a low setting.

This would enable students to access all Web pages on your local network without any difficulties.

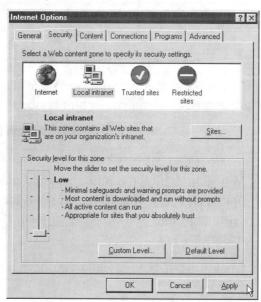

The other settings you want to check are the ***Programs*** options. This tab allows you to set the software applications you frefer to handle different activities. Macintosh users select ***Protocol Helpers*** from ***Preferences*** under the ***Edit*** menu.

Click the ***Programs*** tab.

Click the drop-down menu arrows to select your choices.

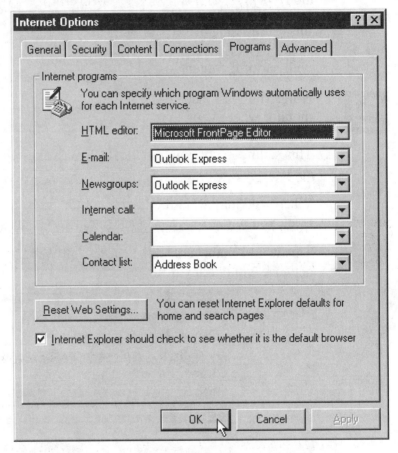

You should click the other tabs and make note of how those options are set. It is always a good idea to be familiar with settings so that you can correct them if your students decide to make changes.

Click the ***OK*** button when you have finished setting your Internet Options.

Exploring the World Wide Web

Now that you have your *Internet Explorer* software set up properly, it is time to start traveling around the World Wide Web. The World Wide Web is that part of the Internet that developed when graphical browsers were introduced to computer users.

The work, which began in 1989, centered on the development of the HyperText Transmission Protocol (HTTP). This is a network protocol for requesting and transmitting Web files and documents which both Web servers and browsers of any computer format can understand. By 1993, browser software was released to the public, and the formation of Web sites has rapidly grown since then.

URLs & Hyperlinks

A URL or Universal Resource Locator references each page on the World Wide Web. This is its Internet address. Once you know an active URL, you can visit that Web page.

 Note: Remember that some URLs are "case sensitive." It makes a difference whether that capital letter should be capitalized or not. Punctuation is also crucial. If you key in the URL incorrectly, you will not go to the correct site. You may not go to any Web site at all.

Time to start visiting some Web pages.

If you know a URL, you can key it into the Address Box. The first Web page you will visit is the **Education Haven**.

1. Key this URL into the Address Box in your *Internet Explorer* window:

   http://www.geocities.com/Athens/1573/educate.html

2. Press the *Enter* key.

You should see this Web page in your browser window. It is a listing of educational Web sites that have been organized into subject categories.

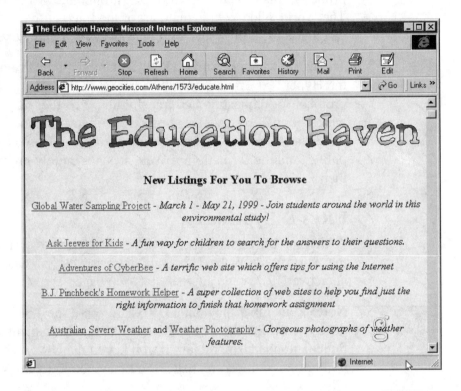

To see more of the list, move the scroll bar on the right-hand side of the Web page up or down. As you move down the list, you will see headings and Web site names.

You should notice that the Web site names are in a different color text and are underlined. They are links to other Web sites. These are called "hypertext links" or "hyperlinks." When you use your mouse to click a hyperlink, your browser will travel to that Web page.

As you scroll down the list, you will see the various categories of Web sites.

Scroll down to the Stories section of the Language Arts category.

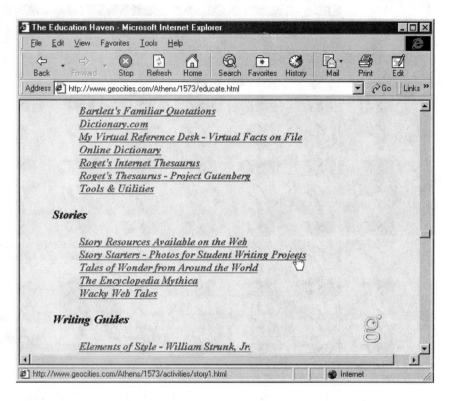

Move your mouse so that it is over the hyperlink:

Story Starters—Photos for Student Writing Projects

You will notice that your cursor changes from the arrow shape to the shape of a small hand. Any time you see the hand shape, your cursor is resting over a hyperlink.

With your cursor over the hyperlink, click once with your left mouse button.

The link will take you to a second Web page containing the Story Starters. This Web page contains photographs that can be used to spark your students' imaginations when they have to create stories.

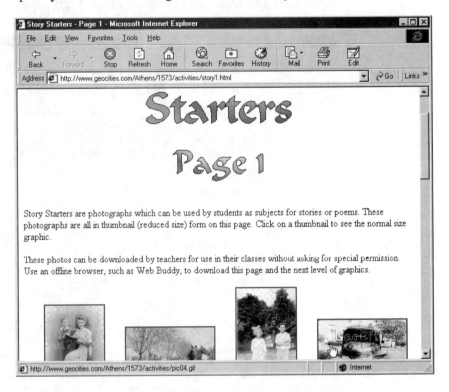

The small photographs on the page are called "thumbnails." They are also hyperlinks. If you move your cursor over them, you will notice it changes to the small hand cursor. You should also notice that the thumbnails have borders around them. This is much like the underlining of text hyperlinks. The border is a clue that the graphic is a link to another Web page.

Move your mouse over the photograph of the old car. Use your left mouse button to click the photograph.

You will see a larger copy of the photograph. Quite often, Web sites will have larger copies of photographs and other graphics available if you click the thumbnail. Thumbnails are quicker for your browser to open.

Sometimes, there will not be a link for you to click to get back to the previous Web page. Click the **Back** button on the Button tool bar to retrace your path.

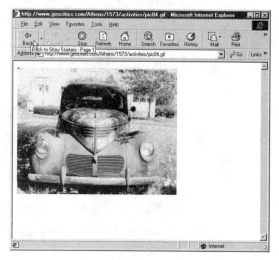

If you scroll further down on the Web page, you will see a graphic that says **Page 2**. It does not have a border around it, but if you move your mouse over it, you will see that your cursor changes to the small hand. This is also a hyperlink that uses a graphic. If you click the **Page 2** hyperlink, you will go to another Web page of photographs.

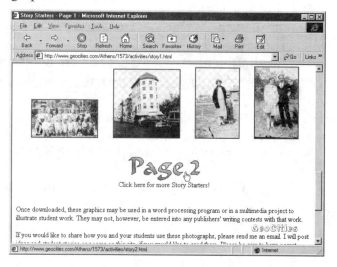

Try visiting **B. J. Pinchbeck's Homework Helper** Web site. A student and his father created it. They wanted to organize a group of Web sites for students to use to help them find answers to homework problems. They have also included some wonderful resource Web sites for teachers.

1. Key this URL into the Address Box:

   http://tristate.pgh.net/~pinch13/

2. Press the *Enter* key.

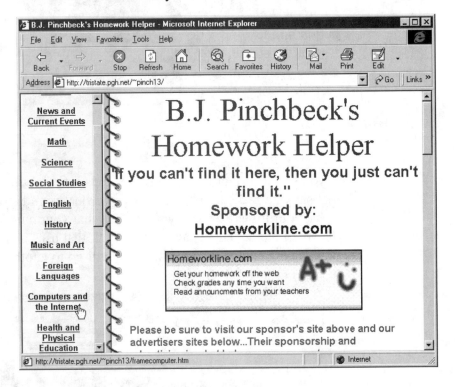

This Web page is divided into sections which are called "frames." There is an index list of hyperlinks in the frame on the left and other informative Web pages are on the right.

3. Click the hyperlink for *Computers and the Internet*.

Once you have clicked the hyperlink, you should see the following Web page. It is a list of other Web pages about Computer Science and the Internet. Sites like **Education Haven** and **B.J. Pinchbeck's Homework Helper** will save you time while searching for related Web sites. They are called index sites where other users share their hours of searching the World Wide Web for information on related topics.

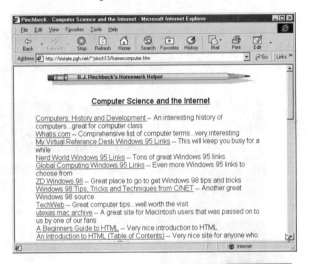

Another way for you to find Web sites is to click the drop-down menu to the right of the *Links* button. Then click the *Quick Search.exe* button.

Follow the instructions given and type your search criteria into the Address Box.

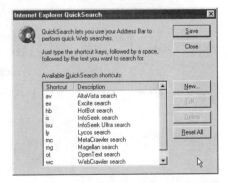

The **Discovery Channel** has a super Web site with content about various topics, classroom activities, and teacher resources, which complements their programming.

1. Key this URL into the Address Box:

   http://discoveryschool.com/

2. Press the ***Enter*** key.

You should see this Web page. It is the beginning or Home page for **Discovery Channel School**. There are some hypertext links and some thumbnail photographs you can use to travel through the Web site. There are also buttons on the left-hand side of the Web page. Buttons are another way for webmasters (people who design Web pages) to lead you to other Web pages.

1. Move your cursor over ***Lesson Plans***.
2. Click that button.

You should now be at the **Discovery School Lesson Plans** Web page. There are many subject areas listed. Each subject is a hyperlink.

1. Move your cursor to *LITERATURE*.
2. Click that hyperlink.

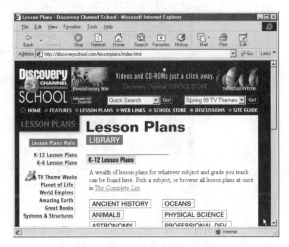

You will see a list of lesson plans related to various works of literature.

3. Scroll down this Web page and move your cursor to *Tales from the Brothers Grimm*.
4. Click that hyperlink.

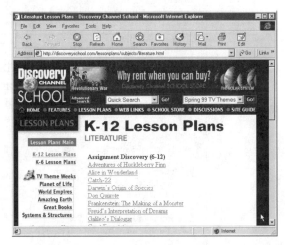

This is an example of what you will find in the lesson plan section. Each lesson plan consists of several parts. You will need to click each hyperlink to read the rest of this lesson.

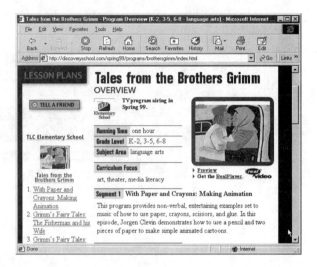

5. Use your *Back* button to return to the **Discovery School** home page.

6. Scroll to the bottom of this Web page. You will see a section called *Search Our Resources*, which is a "search engine" for this Web site. There are many Web pages at this site, and this is another way for you to find what you need.

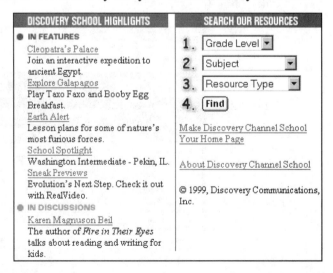

You can click the arrows to select grade levels and topics to meet your criteria.

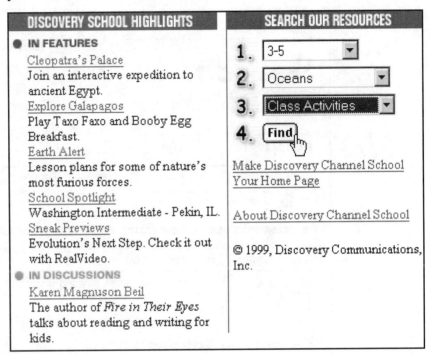

Try this by clicking the arrows to the right of each of the boxes:

1. Choose grade levels *3–5*.
2. Choose the topic *Oceans*.
3. Choose Classroom *Activities*.
4. Click the *Find* button.

Once you click the *Find* button, the search program at this Web site will search through the database of information and send the results back to you on another Web page.

This search shows two resources found. Each site is listed as a hyperlink with a description of what you will find on that Web page.

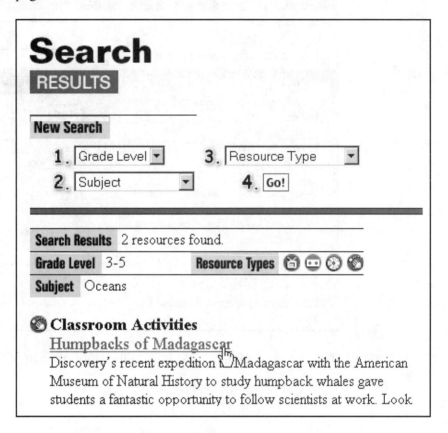

5. Click the hyperlink for ***Humpbacks of Madagascar*** to visit that Web page.

Internet Explorer should take you to this page about the Humpback whales.

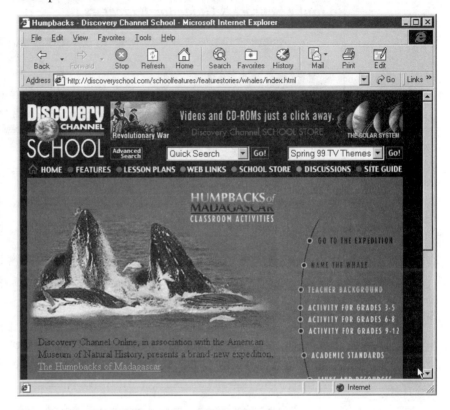

From this page, you can click the **Teacher Background, Activity**, and **Links and Resources** links.

Use the *Back* button on the tool bar to go back to the home page of the **Discovery School** Web site, and click the graphic hyperlink to *Kathy Schrock's Guide for Educators*.

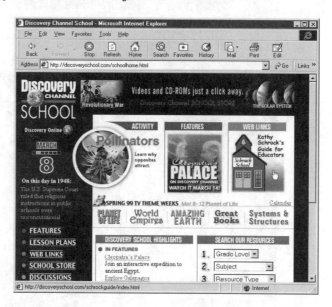

This is another resource Web site that no teacher would want to be without. It is another list of educational Web sites that you can use with your classes.

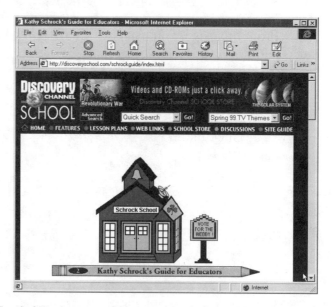

To go directly to this Web page, key the following URL into the Address Box:

http://discoveryschool.com/schrockguide/index.html

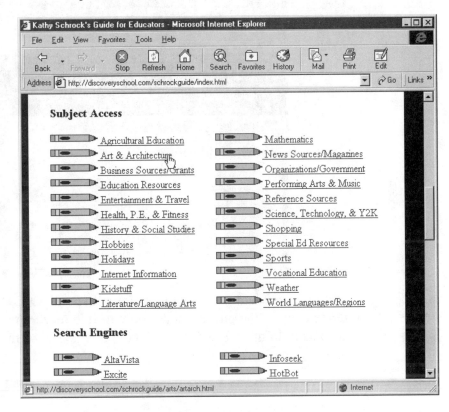

As you scroll down this Web page, you will see various categories of educational Web sites. These are hyperlinks that will take you to the subject lists.

1. Click the *Art & Architecture* link.

Each of the Web sites listed in this guide has a brief explanation written about it. You can click the hyperlinks to visit the listed Web sites.

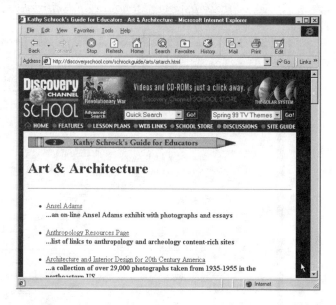

Use the ***Back*** button or click the ***Home*** hyperlink to return to the index page of the guide. Here you will find teacher resources, such as training guides for teachers and slide shows that have been used as training materials.

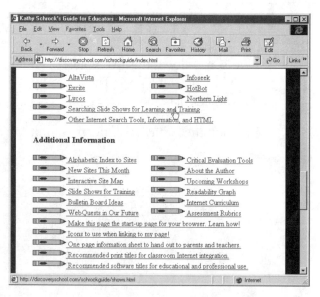

2. Click the ***Searching Slide Shows for Learning and Training*** link.

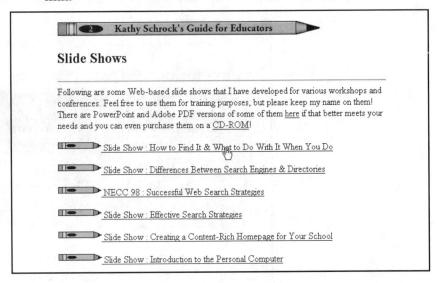

3. To view a sample slide show, click ***Slide Show: How to Find It & What to Do With It When You Do***.

As you can see with this page, not everything on a Web page is formatted in hypertext. There are many programs that allow you to publish your presentations online.

Follow the hyperlinks to move through this slide show.

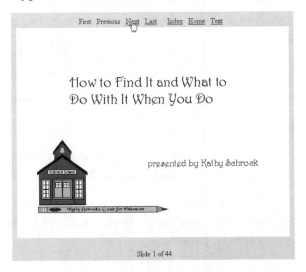

You can use these slide shows as classroom materials, teacher-training modules, or simply as personal training resources.

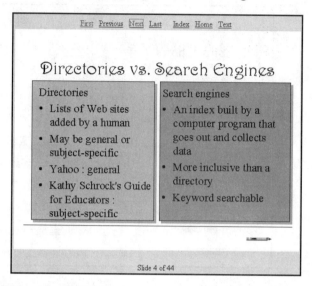

This particular slide show teaches you how to find information on the World Wide Web.

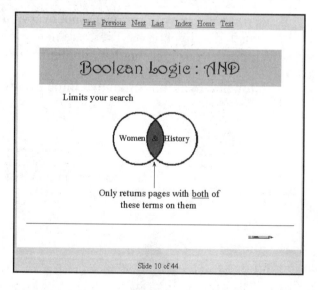

There are tips on how to successfully search for information. It also gives you suggestions for using some of that information once you have found it.

Another site for you and your students to visit is **MidLink Magazine**. This is a digital magazine created for kids, by kids. First created by students at Ligon GT Magnet Middle School in Raleigh, North Carolina, MidLink Magazine has grown into a digital magazine for students all over the world.

1. Key this URL into the Address Box:

   http://longwood.cs.ucf.edu/~MidLink/

2. Press the *Enter* key.

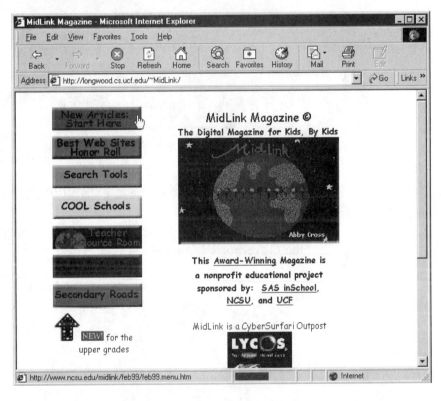

This will take you to the current issue of **MidLink Magazine**. You will see several hypertext links that will lead you to information about the project's sponsors. You will find the graphic hyperlinks on the left-hand side of the Web page.

3. Click the *New Articles: Start Here* button.

One of this issue's projects is called Monu-MENTAL. The project
was designed for other schools to send in their results and become
part of the process of sharing information via the Internet.

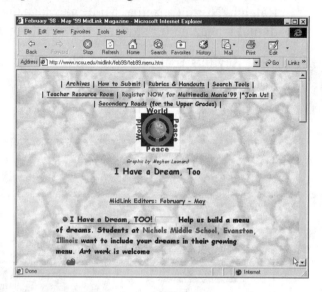

4. Click ***Monu-MENTAL*** to see some of the projects already
   online.

5. Click ***Durant Road Middle School*** to see how they shared
   the Governor's Mansion with the world.

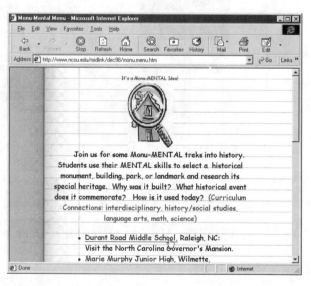

6. Click the hyperlink, *Click here to See Slides*, to visit their project.

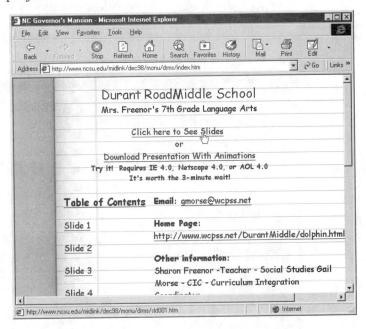

7. To navigate through this slide show, click the buttons

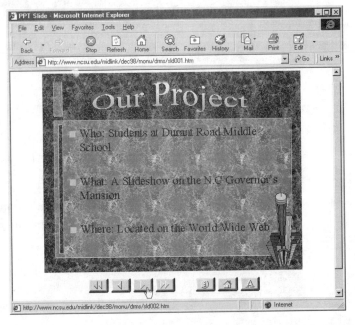

To visit another Web site created for educators and students:

1. Key this URL into the Address Box:

   http://www.gsn.org/index.html

2. Press the *Enter* key.

The **Global Schoolhouse** began back in 1984 with the FrEdMail (Free Educational) Network. This was a program in which students from various locations could participate in e-mail (electronic mail) projects with each other.

Today there are a wide variety of activities you and your students can join. A quick way to see this assortment is to go to the *Site At A Glance* Web page.

3. Click the *Site At A Glance* button on the left-hand side of the Web page.

You will see this index page which gives you many ways to find information available on the Web site.

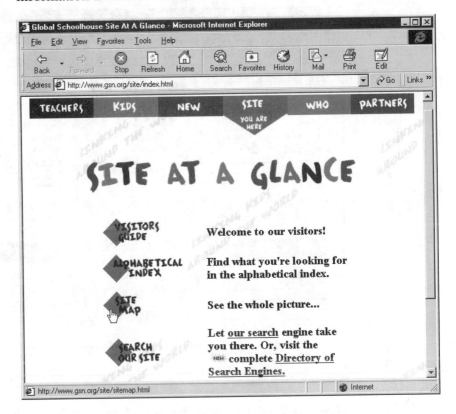

4. Click the *Site Map* hyperlink.

This will take you to an easy-to-view map of all of the topics covered in this Web site.

This Web page shows various topics that are divided into groups. Although the text is not a different color and is not underlined, each title is a hyperlink to a Web page. As you move your cursor over the text, you will notice the small hand appear.

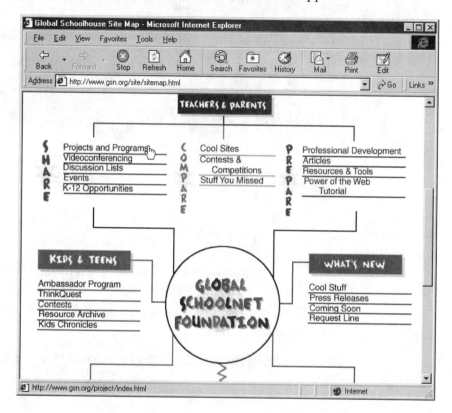

There are sections about sharing information, preparing to use the Internet, new activities or announcements, information about The Global SchoolNet Foundation, and partnerships with other companies and organizations.

5. Click *Projects and Programs*.

This link will take you to a list of the current projects available for your classes to join.

6. Click the ***GeoGame*** hyperlink to see one of the activities. The GeoGame started as an e-mail project, but now has a "Web" format.

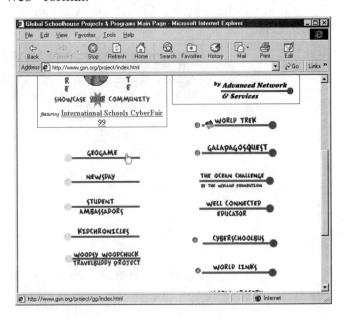

7. Click ***Project Description*** to read more about the game.
8. Click ***Play a Game*** to continue.

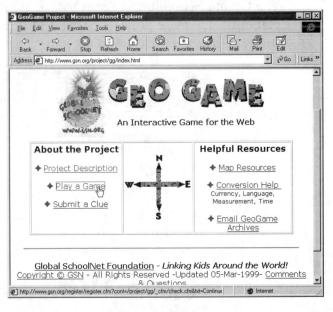

If you have not registered with **Global Schoolhouse** to participate in any other projects, click the hyperlink for new participants.

You will be asked to fill in your real name and address when you register.

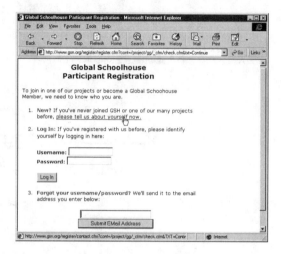

9. When you are registered and ready to participate, fill in your "Log In" information.

10. Then click the ***Log In*** button.

The **Global Schoolhouse** keeps a database of everyone who participates in these projects. This is to safeguard you and your students from people who do not participate properly.

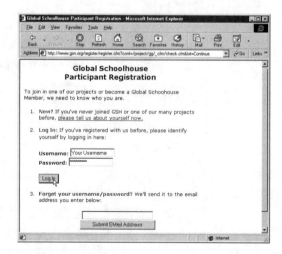

Once the Web site recognizes you as a registered participant, you can either choose to play a game or submit your own clues. Take a look at some sets of clues before you enter any of your own.

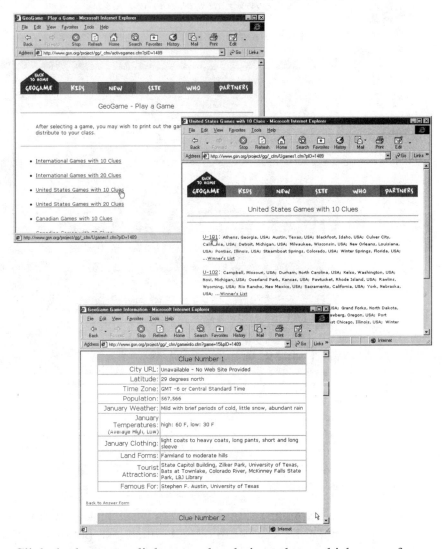

Click the hypertext links to make choices about which type of game you want your students to play. You will then see a set of clues to locations in the United States, Canada, or the World. Your students can solve these puzzles, and you can submit their responses. This is a super activity even if you are not participating online.

Another type of hyperlink site map is an Image Map.

1. Key this URL into your Address Box.

   http://www.ars.usda.gov/is/kids/

2. Press the **Enter** key.

The United States Department of Agriculture has a **Sci4Kids** Web site full of activities to help children learn about scientists and agriculture.

When you see this Web site's home page, you do not see any hyperlinks. Instead of underlined text, buttons, or individual graphics to click, you see one big graphic image that is divided into "invisible" hyperlinks.

3. Click the silly-faced Venus Flytrap under the magnifying glass.

As the silly face on that Venus Flytrap might have suggested, this hyperlink takes you to the **Weird Science** Web page.

This Web page supplies scientific answers to weird questions asked by kids.

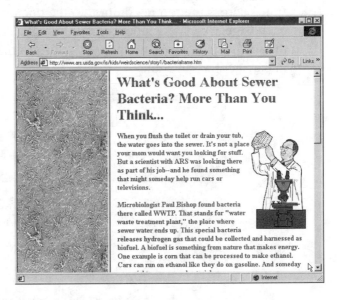

4. Click the question and follow that hyperlink to the answer Web page.

At the main menu, selecting the scientist with the light bulb head hyperlink allows your students to find out information about various types of scientists.

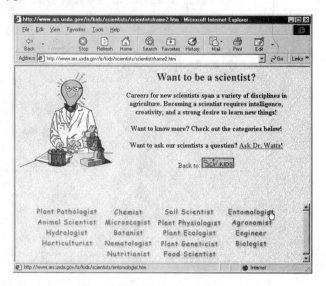

This is also a Web page that is divided into frames. There is a frame across the top in addition to the one across the bottom of each page. As your students read through the information about the scientists, they do not have to return to the starting page to make another selection.

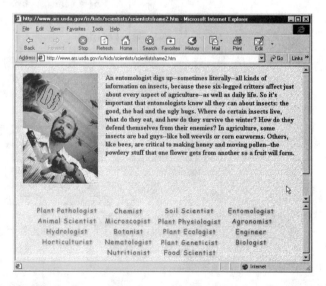

Another site with an example of an Image Map is the **National Weather Service** Web site.

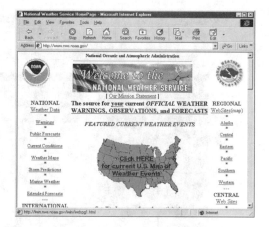

1. Key this URL into the Address Box.

   http://www.nws.noaa.gov/

2. Press the ***Enter*** key.

3. Click the graphic of the United States to go to a Web page with a "clickable" map of the states.

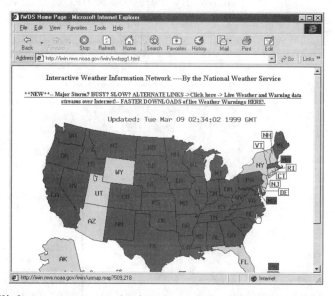

4. Click your state on the image map to find information about its current weather patterns.

Each state also has an image map showing cities that have local weather reports available.

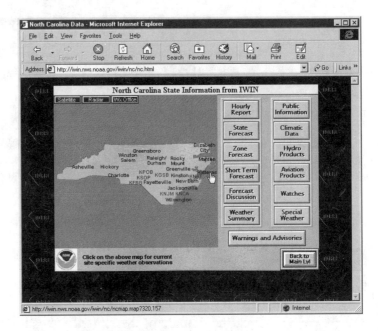

5. Click a city name to see the report Web page.

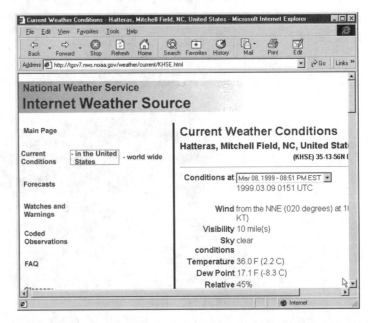

What will happen when you enter an incorrect URL, or the hyperlink you click is incorrect, or the Web page no longer exists? You will see one of a variety of error messages.

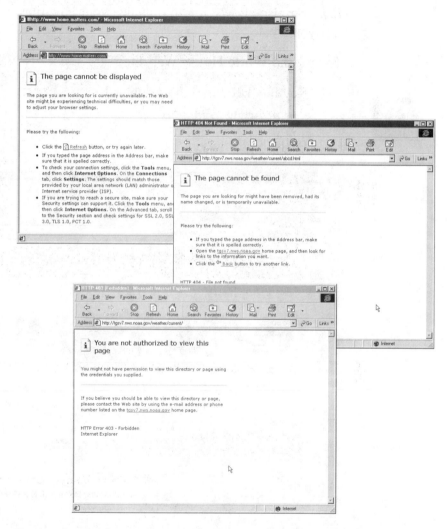

Do not let the language used in the error message scare you. It is not personal. These are stock messages that are delivered by a network computer to let you know the Web page URL you have tried to access does not exist.

Check your spelling, capitalization, and punctuation first. If those are all correct, then perhaps the Web page no longer exists.

Favorites

When you find Web sites that you do not want to lose, you can create a "favorite" link for an easy way back to that site. *Internet Explorer* also allows you to organize your Favorites into folders that you create.

To visit the **White House** Web site:

1. Key this URL into the Address Box.

   http://www.whitehouse.gov

2. Press the *Enter* key.

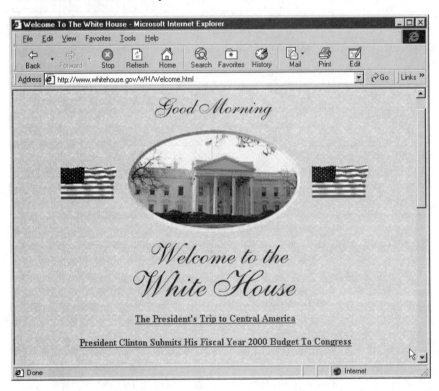

Notice that the URL in your Address Box changes to:

    http://www.whitehouse.gov/WH/Welcome.html

The White House computer changes this automatically as it leads you to the welcome Web page.

You may find it difficult to remember different URLs. By creating Favorites you will not have to remember them or write them down.

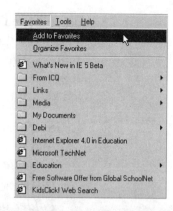

There are several ways to create your Favorites folder.

1. Click *Favorites*.
2. Click *Add to Favorites*.
3. Click the *OK* button on the *Add Favorite* dialog box.
4. Click the *Favorites* button to see your list of favorite Web sites.

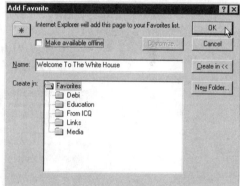

If you think about this method for a minute, you will realize that if you start marking every interesting site as a favorite, you can rapidly collect a long list.

In order to keep your Favorites folder organized, *Internet Explorer* allows you to create individual folders. You can see several folders already created as soon as you install *Internet Explorer*.

You will need to create individual Favorites folders before you can put Web sites into them.

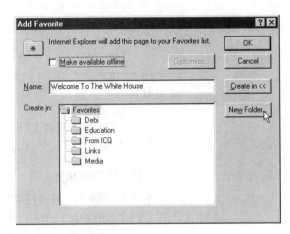

5. Select *Favorites*, *Add to Favorites*.

6. Click the *New Folder button*.

7. Key *School* into the *Folder name:* box.

8. Click the *OK* button.

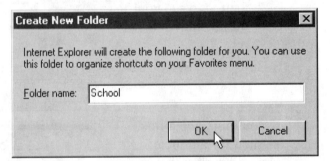

Now that you have created the folder, you can save Web sites into it.

9. Click the *School* folder to select it.

10. Click the *OK* button to put the White House favorite into it.

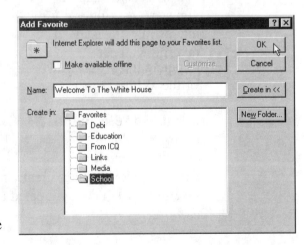

Now take a look at your new Favorites list.

11. Click **Favorites**.

12. Click the **School** folder.

You should see your new favorite in the School folder.

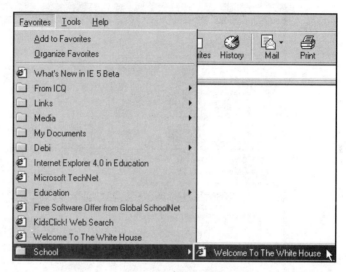

In your classroom, you can make a Favorites folder for each student or team of students using the computer. As they find Web sites that interest them, they can file the favorites into their folders.

To delete the original favorite for the **White House**:

1. Click **Favorites**.

2. Click **Organize Favorites** to open the organizing utility.

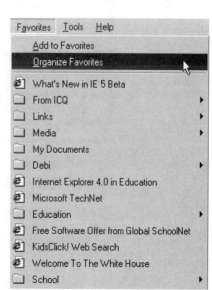

3. Click the Favorite listing for the White House once to highlight it.

4. Click the **Delete** button.

5. Click the **Close** button to close this utility.

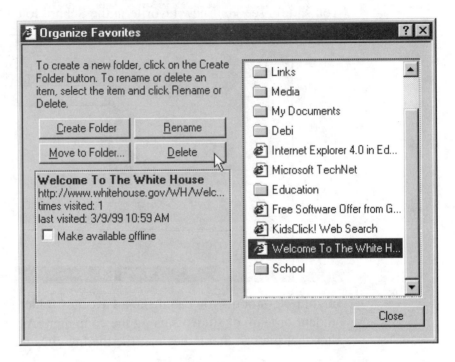

6. Click the **Yes** button to confirm deletion of that favorite.

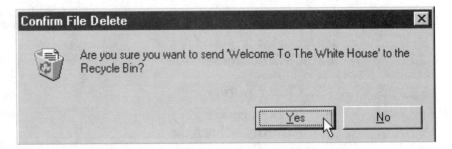

You have now successfully deleted that favorite from your list.

Click the *Favorites* button to check your list.

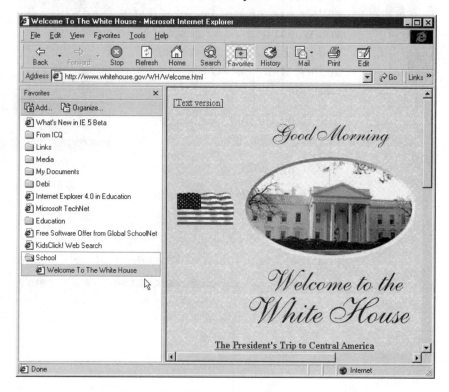

You should see that the single entry for the White House is now gone.

Continue to add favorites to your folders as you find sites you want to remember. Once you have those favorite sites marked, it is easy to go back to visit them.

1. Click the *Favorites* button.
2. Click the folder you want to open.
3. Click the Web page you want to visit.
4. Click the *X* button to close the Favorites list and see the full web page.

Note: If you work at home and collect a number of favorites that you would like to use at school, you can export the list to a disk and use it in your school computer.

The Export utility can be found in your *File* menu.

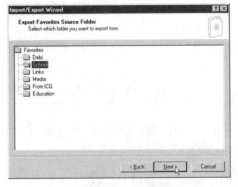

1. Click *File*.
2. Click *Import and Export*.

3. Follow the Export Wizard directions.
4. Select the folder of Favorites you want to save to disk.

5. Save the file to a disk, and then you can use it on any other computer.

Remember: The instructions for using the Export utility are in the *File Menu* section of this book (page 18).

Printing Web Pages

In this section, you will learn how to print Web pages on paper.

You can use the **White House** Web site in this example.

1. Key this URL into the Address Box in *Internet Explorer*:
   http://www.whitehouse.gov

2. Press the ***Enter*** key.

3. Scroll down the Web page until you see these menu choices.

4. Click the ***White House History and Tours:*** link.

5. Click The *Presidents of the United States*.

6. Select *George Washington*.

There is a Web page about each president. This can be useful information for your Social Studies class, or it can be used as a template design for a project about mathematicians, scientists, or authors.

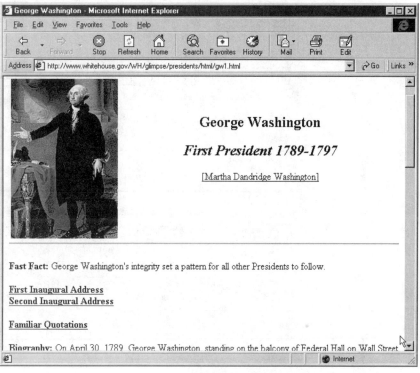

Before printing, you will need to check your page setup.

7. Click *File*.
8. Click *Page Setup*.

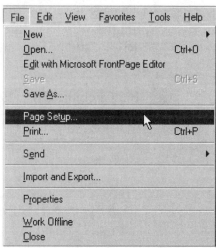

9. Make sure that the page is set the way you want it to print.

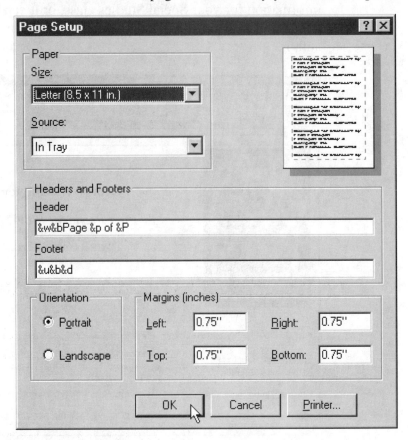

This page is set for ³/₄-inch margins all around the page. It will print the Web page title and page numbers in the header. The URL, location of the information, and the current date will print in the footer.

10. Click the **OK** button to confirm the setup.

11. Click *File* and *Print* when you are ready to print the Web pages.

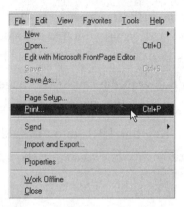

12. Instead of clicking *File* and *Print*, you can click the *Print* button on your toolbar.

13. When the printer dialog box appears, check your settings for number of copies, etc. and click the *OK* button.

Note: Make sure the correct printer has been selected.

Saving Web Pages

There are many reasons to save a Web page. You can use it as a template file for creating a page of your own. You can print it to share with your students. Or you may simply want to use the Web page with an overhead or LCD projector as part of a lesson.

Practice with the same Web page about George Washington. To quickly find that page, use this URL:

1. Key this URL into the Address Box.

http://www.whitehouse.gov/WH/glimpse/presidents/html/gw1.html

2. Press the ***Enter*** key.

You should see this Web page about George Washington.

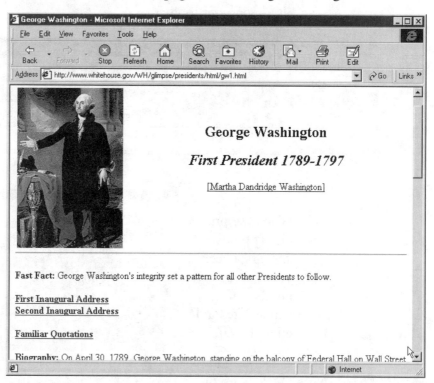

3. Click *File*.
4. Click *Save As*.

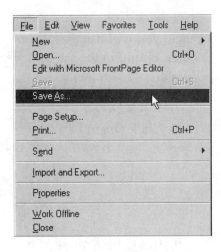

5. In the *Save As* dialog box, select a disk or folder location.
6. Click the *Save* button.

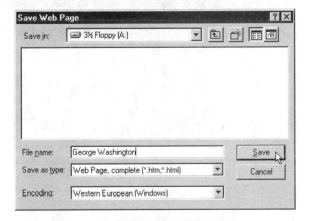

As the file is saving, you will see this dialog box showing the percentage of the file that has been saved.

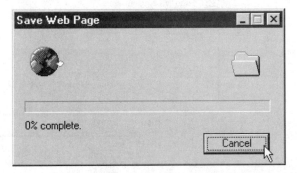

To view a saved Web page, you will use the ***Open*** option in the ***File*** drop-down menu.

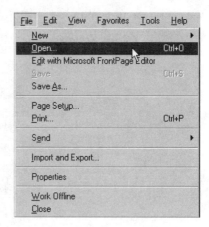

7. Click ***File***.
8. Click ***Open***.

9. Click the ***Browse*** button to browse and find the file you want to open.

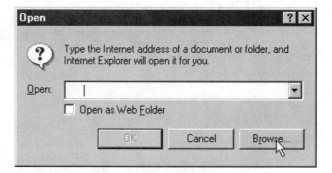

10. Select the file you want to open.
11. Click the ***Open*** button.

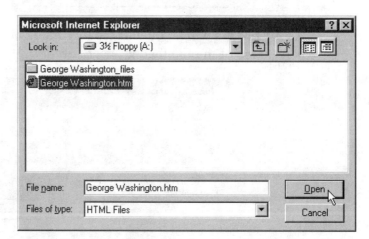

12. Click the *OK* button on the *Open* dialog box.

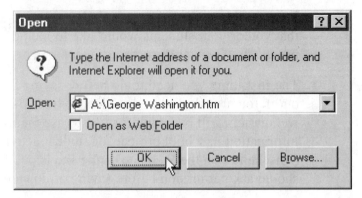

You will now see the **George Washington** Web page. You have saved the HTML formatting with the text and graphics.

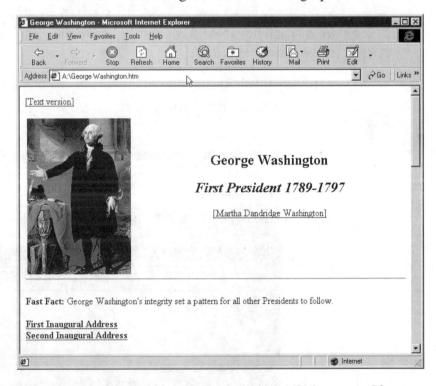

This process will work for saving individual Web pages. If you also want attached multimedia files and additional Web pages, you can use an offline browser program, such as *Web Buddy*, to download groups of pages.

Saving Files from Web Pages

There will be times when you find a photograph or graphic image that you or your students would like to include in a multimedia presentation or word-processed document.

The first thing you need to do before saving the image is to find out if you are allowed to download it from the Web page. Many webmasters will be happy for you to use their images and information in school projects or student activities. Unless there is a disclaimer on the Web site or the site is public information, you should ask permission before saving or downloading it.

Once you know you can download the image, there are a few simple steps you can follow.

You can use some images from the **Earth from Space** Web site for this activity. NASA allows the use of their photographs for any educational project.

1. Key this URL into the Address Box and press the *Enter* key.

   http://earth.jsc.nasa.gov/

2. Click the *Clickable Map* hyperlink.

The photograph gallery is divided into major topics.

3. Click the ***Hurricanes and Weather*** button in the lower left corner.

4. From the ***Search*** menu, scroll down and select ***Hurricanes***.
5. Click the ***Start Search*** button.

You may have to wait a few minutes for the graphics and information to load when you make choices at this Web site. Some topics have more possible graphics than others do.

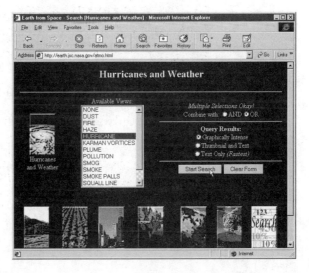

In this instance, there is only one photograph in the database at this time. It is a photo of Hurricane Elena in the Gulf of Mexico. You will see an option to select a Hi-Resolution photo or a Lo-Resolution photo. Unless you have a very fast Internet connection, do NOT select Hi-Resolution. The photos are larger than what you would need for most projects and will take a long time to download.

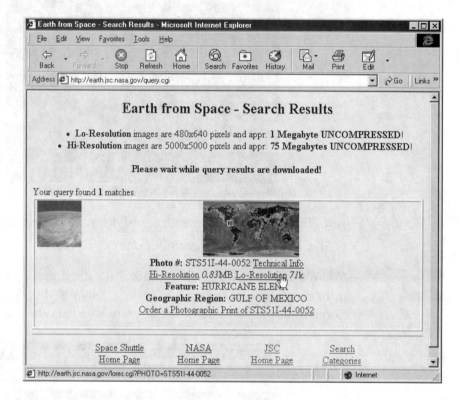

6. Click the *Lo-Resolution* hypertext link.

You will need to wait just a few minutes for the graphic to fully load into your browser.

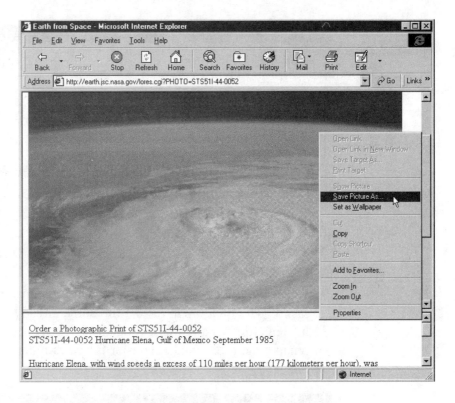

You will see that this database has information about each photograph in a separate frame in your *Internet Explorer* window. You may want to print this information or have your students take notes from it while you are at the Web page.

In order to save the photograph to a folder on your hard drive or to a diskette, follow these steps.

7. Right-click the photograph.
8. On the menu that pops up, select ***Save Picture As***.

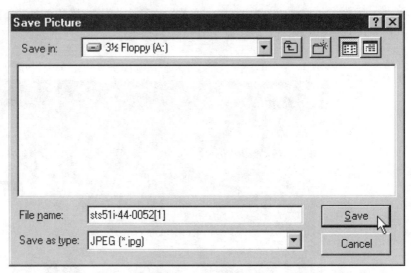

9. Select the folder or disk location where the image will be saved. The image will have a file name already assigned to it. This file has a numerical database file name. You can rename the file to make it easier for you to identify each image.

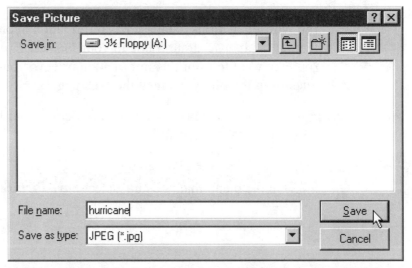

10. Renaming this file to *hurricane* will help you remember that it is the hurricane photograph. You can also name it *Elena*.

11. Click the *Save* button when you are ready to save the photograph file.

Once you have saved an image, you can transport it to another computer and use it in different programs that can use that image format.

Images used in Web pages are usually either GIF (Graphics Interchange Format) or JPG/JPEG (Joint Photographic Experts Group) format.

In order to view a GIF or JPG graphic, you can use *Internet Explorer*.

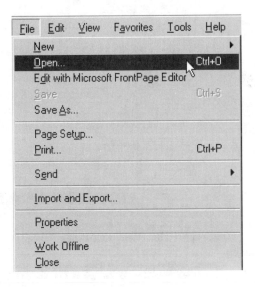

12. Click *File*.
13. Click *Open Page*.
14. Click the *Browse* button on the *Open* dialog box.

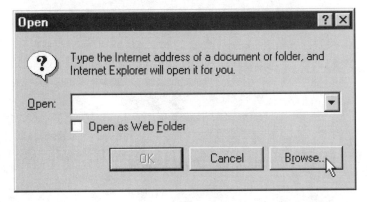

15. In the ***Open*** dialog box, click to view the ***Files of type:*** drop-down menu. Select ***All Files*** so that you can see graphics files as well as the HTML files.

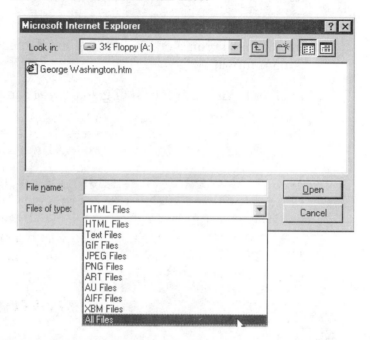

16. Select the ***hurricane.jpg*** file that was saved.

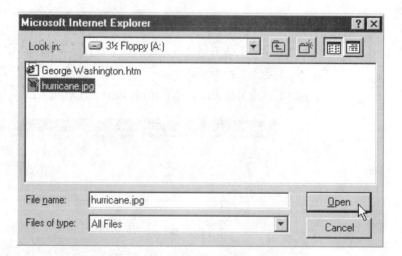

17. Click the ***Open*** button.

18. Click the *OK* button on the *Open* dialog box.

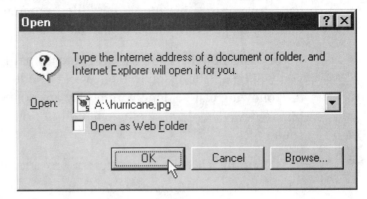

You should now see the hurricane photograph image in your *Internet Explorer* window. If you have another graphics program, you can resize this image and change the file type for use in a multimedia program. Many of the new programs are accepting GIF or JPG graphics as file formats, so you may not have to change the file type.

Graphic images are not the only files that can be saved to your hard drive or to a diskette. Sound files, program files, and multimedia program files can also be saved.

If you visit the **Kid's and Youth Educational Page** from the FBI, you will be able to listen to their weekly Radio Show. However the following can be done with nearly any sound file. See http://www.yahooligans.com/content/d/ for other appropriate sound files.

1. Key this URL into the Address Box and press the *Enter* key:

   http://www.fbi.gov/kids/kids.htm

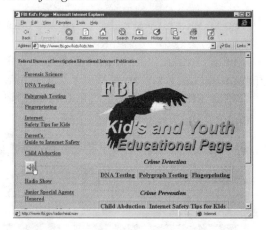

Click the sound button to hear a recorded message from the Radio Show.

You may see the *Windows Media Player* or *Apple QuickTime* open and play the sound file as it downloads.

3. You can also click the hypertext link just below the button to read a transcript of the sound file.

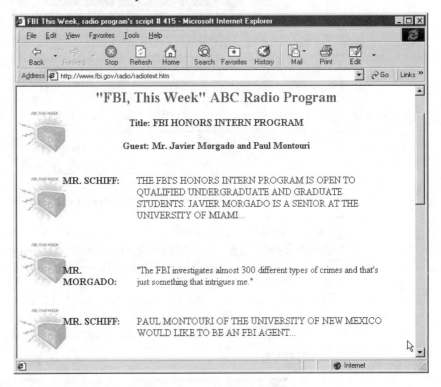

4. To save this (or any other sound file) right-click the button or hyperlink. Macintosh users click and hold.

You will see this pop-up menu appear.

5. Click *Save Target As* (Windows). *Download Link to Disk* (Macintosh).

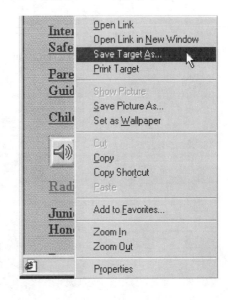

6. Select the folder or diskette where the file will be saved.

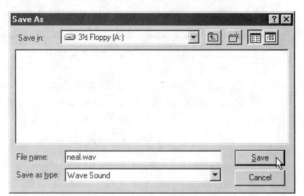

7. Click the *Save* button on the *Save As* dialog box.

The file is now saved and can be played on any computer with a sound player. This type of program usually comes with your sound card. You can also open the file in *Internet Explorer*.

The FBI Kids Web site also has instructional material about DNA testing, fingerprinting, polygraph testing, and other topics. The fingerprinting Web page has super images of the basic types of fingerprints.

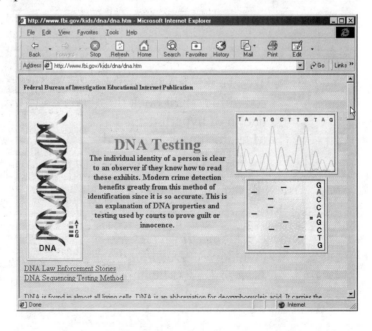

You can also save movie files from Web sites to use on your computer at school as part of your lessons. *QuickTime* movies (.mov or .qt files) can be used in *HyperStudio* cards as part of a student's multimedia presentation.

Saving movie files to your hard drive greatly reduces the time you and your students will have to wait for the file to download from the Internet.

For example, the **Federal Emergency Management Agency** has a Web site for students.

1. Key this URL into the Address Box and press the *Enter* key:

   http://www.fema.gov/kids/

You should see the **FEMA for Kids** Web page.

There are many games and puzzles for students to use to learn how to prepare for emergencies.

2. Click the **Main Icons** graphic hyperlink at the bottom of the page to go to a main index page.

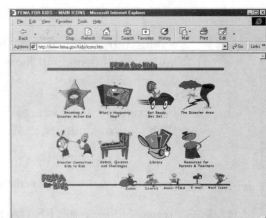

3. Click the **Library** graphic hyperlink to go to the resources archives.

4. Click the hyperlink for the **Video** resources in the Library.

There are *RealMedia* and *QuickTime* movie files available for you to view.

RealMedia files will be discussed in the Helper Applications section of this book.

5. Scroll down the page until you find the hyperlink for the *QuickTime Tornado* video.

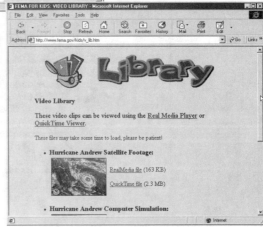

6. Right-click the hyperlink for the *QuickTime* file (Windows), click and hold (Macintosh).

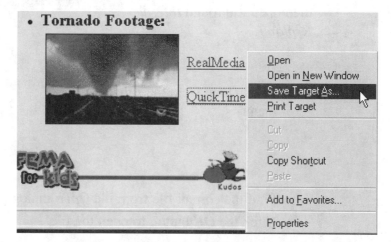

7. Select ***Save Target As*** (Windows) or ***Download to Disk*** (Macintosh) from the pop-up menu.

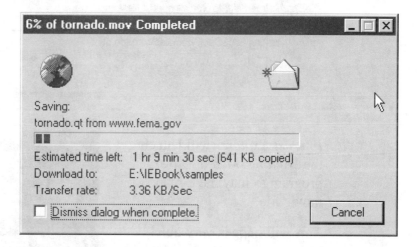

The download time from the Internet for a 33.6 modem is about an hour. This would not be a very useful lesson for your students if you had to wait an hour for the file to appear on your computer.

Once you have saved the movie file to your hard drive, you can then open it through *Internet Explorer*.

8. Click **Open** from the **File** menu.

9. Find the correct file from the **Open** dialog box.

10. Click the **OK** button to open the file.

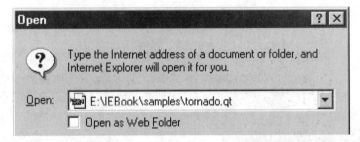

Internet Explorer will launch the *Windows Media Player* program to play the tornado movie file.

This will happen very quickly so that you and your students will be able to view it without waiting for an hour. You can also use the Play, Pause, and Stop features of the player.

Using Plug-Ins

Plug-Ins are programs that you download from the World Wide Web. They work within *Internet Explorer* to help you view special files such as movie files and virtual reality files.

One such plug-in is the *QuickTime* movie viewer from Apple Computer, Inc. This plug-in is used to view .mov movie files.

1. Key this URL into the Address Box and press the ***Enter*** key.

   http://starchild.gsfc.nasa.gov/docs/StarChild/StarChild.html

It will take you to the welcome Web page for the **StarChild** site.

2. Click the ***Level 2 Solar System*** hyperlink.

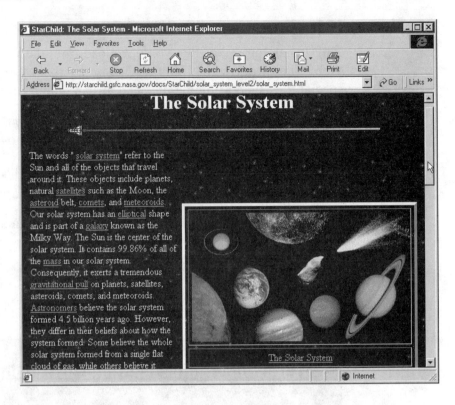

There are many hypertext links on these Web pages that will take you to additional information about the Solar System.

3. Scroll down the page until you find the links for the movies.

There are two movies available, an AVI format movie and a *QuickTime* (MOV) format movie. In order for you to play the *QuickTime* movie, you must have the *QuickTime* plug-in installed.

You can find it at the Apple Computer, Inc. Web site:

http://www.apple.com/quicktime/

Follow the directions for downloading and installing the plug-in program.

Once you have the plug-in installed, you can view the *QuickTime* movie.

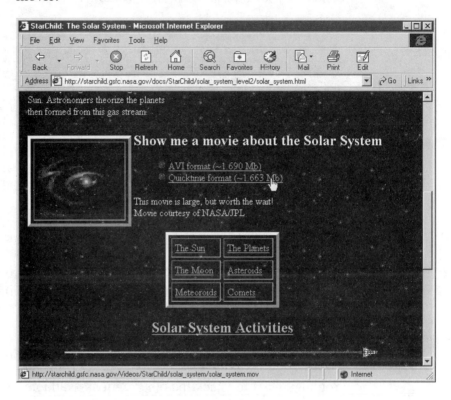

4. Click the hypertext link for the *QuickTime* format movie.

If you do not have the *QuickTime* plug-in installed correctly, you may see this graphic image in your *Internet Explorer* window. This means that the file cannot play or that the file did not download correctly.

Until the download is complete, you will see this icon in the center of your *Internet Explorer* window.

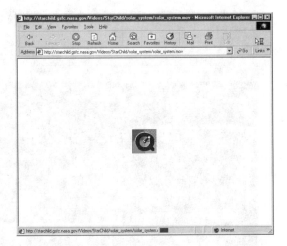

5. Right-click (Windows), click and hold (Macintosh) the *Internet Explorer* window to adjust the size of the movie once it starts to play.

6. Click **Zoom**.

7. Select the appropriate video size to view the movie.

You may want to check the other options available for movie viewing.

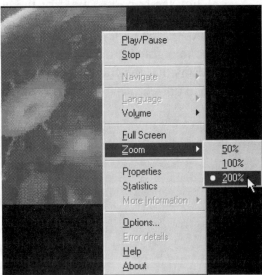

When the download is complete and you have set your video size, you will see the movie appear in the center of your *Internet Explorer* window.

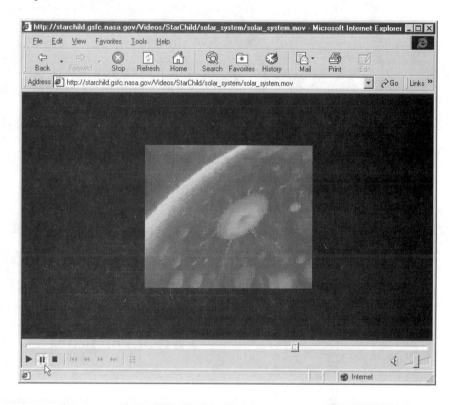

You can use the *QuickTime* controls at the bottom of your *Internet Explorer* window to control sound, playing/pausing, and fast forwarding or rewinding.

Another plug-in program is the *Cosmo VRML* player by CosmoSoftware. It is designed to play VRML (Virtual Reality Modeling Language) files. The program can be downloaded from the CosmoSoftware Web site.

http://cosmosoftware.com/

Once you have installed the player, you can visit many Web sites with virtual reality interactive graphics. Here are some examples of what you and your students will find.

The **Virtual Polyhedra** site has a variety of geometric shapes that your students can view from all sides by manipulating the image in the viewer.

1. The site is at the URL:

   http://www.li.net/%7Egeorge/virtual-polyhedra/vp.html

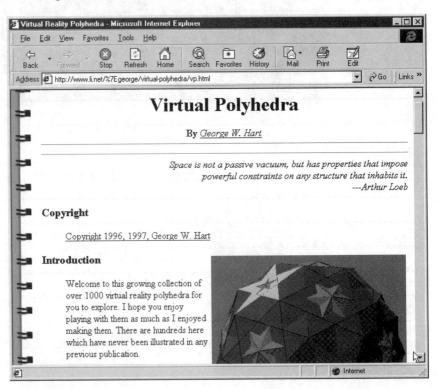

There are geometric shapes in a variety of categories.

2. Click one of the lists of models.

3. Click an image name to open that file.

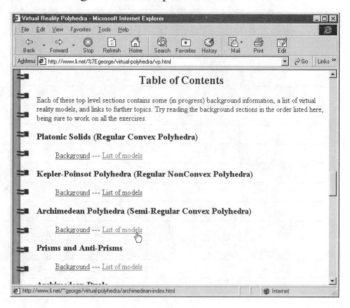

4. Once the image is loaded, you can rotate, zoom in, spin, and tilt it using the *Cosmo* plug-in program.

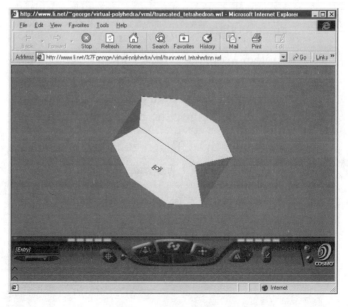

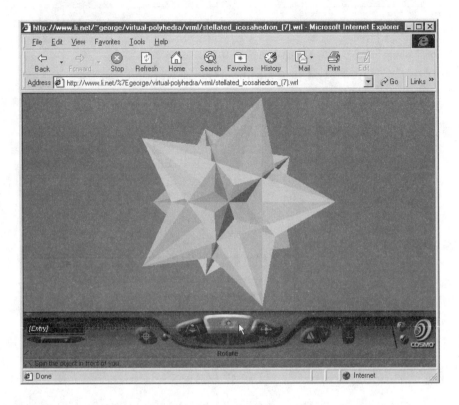

From simple objects to this more elaborate shape, the images are a terrific resource for any math class. There is also background information about the images and instructions for making some paper models.

Another Web site with geometric shapes for students to manipulate is the **MathMol K-12 Activity Page**. There are hypermedia textbooks, and a quick tour of the Web site. Your students will enjoy the 3-D model images.

1. Enter this URL to go to the Web site.

   http://www.nyu.edu/pages/mathmol/K_12.html

The **MathMol** site has molecular and geometric models for you and your students to manipulate.

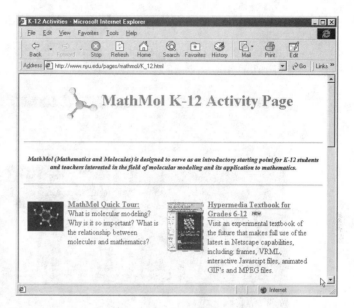

2. Scroll down the Web page until you find the hypertext links for the libraries of Geometric and Molecular structures.

3. Click the *Library of 3-D Geometric Structures* hyperlink.

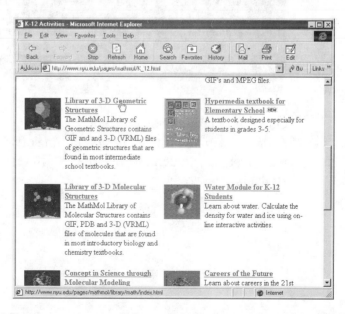

There are plane surfaces such as circle, triangle, or rectangle. These are good examples to show two-dimensional surfaces.

4. Click the ***3-D Figures Library*** hyperlink on this page.

There are 3-D shapes such as a cone, dodecahedron, cube, cylinder, and sphere.

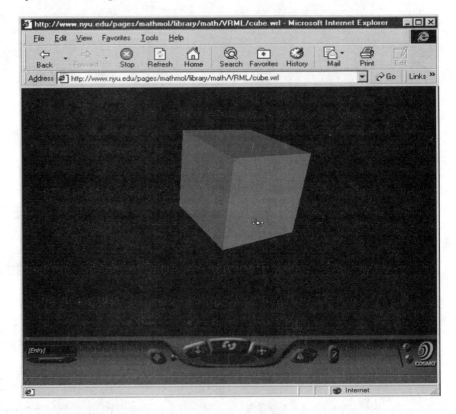

Once you make a choice, the object will appear in your *Internet Explorer* window if the *Cosmo* plug-in software is working. This is a super way to demonstrate many different shapes to your students.

The *Library of 3-D Molecular Structures* has a database for Water and Ice, Carbons, Hydrocarbons, Molecules of Life, and Drugs.

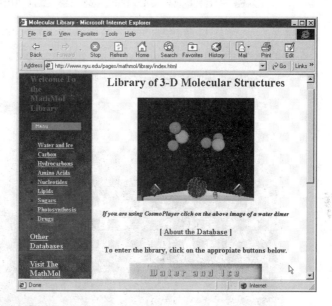

5. Select *Water and Ice* to view those molecules. This part of the Web site offers your students a chance to manipulate molecular models.

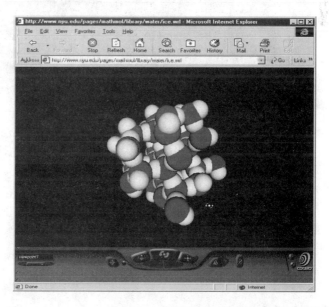

Another Web site with 3-D VRML files is the **Earth in VRML** Web site.

1. Key the URL into the Address Box and press the *Enter* key.

   http://vrml.gsfc.nasa.gov/

This Web site contains various images of the Earth that will allow your students to take a different look at our planet.

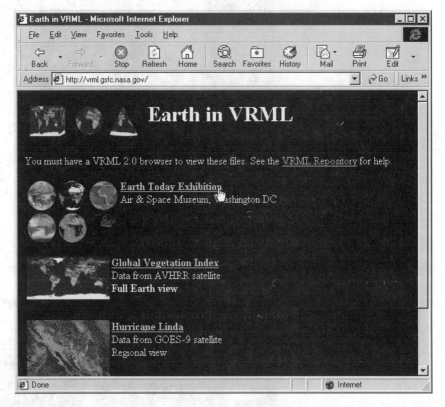

2. Click the hyperlink for the *Earth Today Exhibition*. This will take you to a Web page with viewing choices for the earth models.

3. If you want all six globes to appear in your *Internet Explorer* window, select the three across, two down view option.

You will see six views of Earth. There is a normal view from space taken from the Galileo Spacecraft, one for ocean temperatures, one for the Earth's crust, and several others.

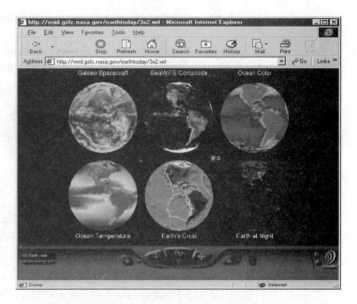

You can zoom in on any of the models. You can even spin and rotate them so that your view is from the top, bottom, or any angle from Earth's normal rotation.

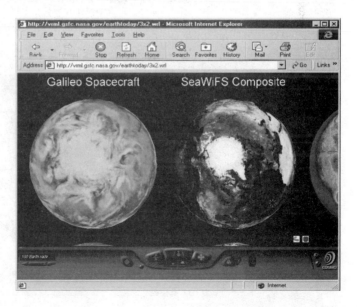

The ***Global Vegetation Index*** shows an image of the Earth with vegetation areas in different colors. Your students can view any of the continents from a variety of angles.

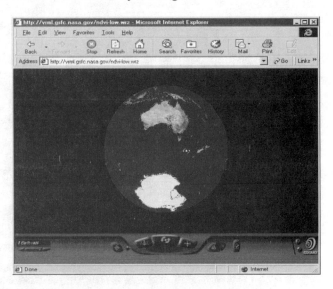

The hyperlink for ***Hurricane Linda*** images will link you to a Web page with several types of images of this hurricane.

4. Select the VRML image so that your students can manipulate the 3-D model of a hurricane.

If you are teaching a unit about the Solar System, you might want to take your students to this Web site.

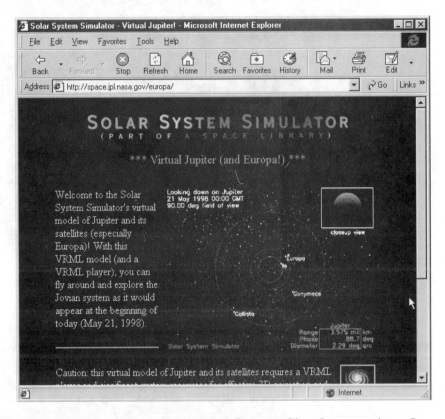

This Web page is part of the **Solar System Simulator** project. It is called Virtual Jupiter (and Europa!). You can find it at the URL:

http://space.jpl.nasa.gov/europa/

Your students will be able to manipulate Jupiter and its moons in the VRML viewer. This will give them an opportunity to view the orbits of the moons from different angles.

1. Once you go to the Web site, click the hyperlink *Show me Virtual Jupiter!*

2. Each satellite (or moon) is labeled and is shown on its orbital path. Your students can zoom in on the planet.

3. They can even zoom in on the satellites to see the various surfaces.

The Jupiter model is the only VRML file at this site, but there are many other images your students can view or create at the **Solar System Simulator** main Web page.

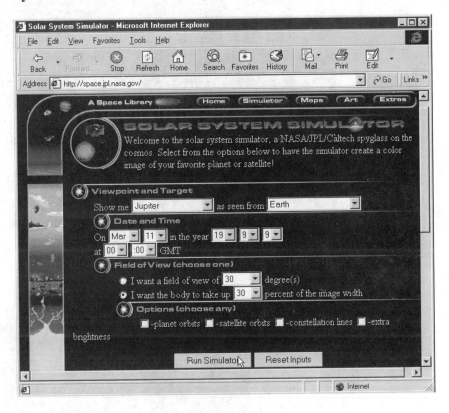

1. Click the hyperlink from the Jupiter page or key in this URL to go to the **Solar System Simulator**.

   http://space.jpl.nasa.gov/

2. Select the object you wish to view and the location from which you want to view it.

3. Next select the date and the time of the observation. You can also include planet and satellite orbits if you wish.

4. Click the ***Run Simulation*** button.

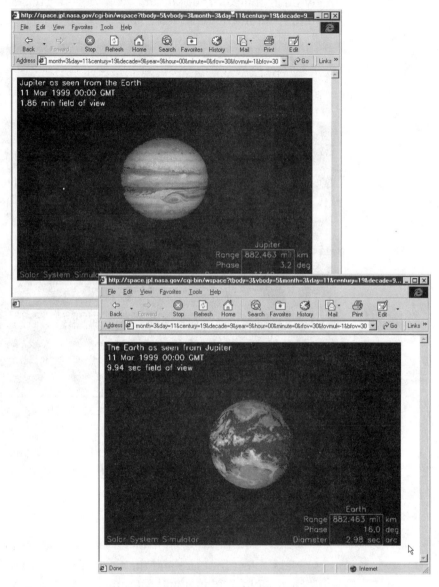

The simulation program will generate a photographic image with your specifications.

5. You can then save that image to your hard drive or a diskette following the directions for saving a graphic.

Another Web site to visit, if you are teaching about the planets, is the **Mars Pathfinder** Web site. It also has virtual reality models so you and your students can view where the Pathfinder landed and where the Rover traveled on the surface of Mars.

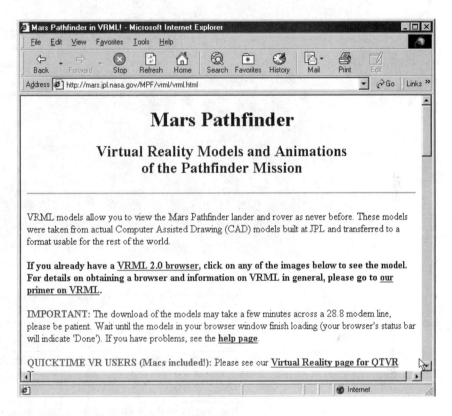

1. The **Mars Pathfinder** in VRML Web site is located at the URL:

   http://mars.jpl.nasa.gov/MPF/vrml/vrml.html

2. Scroll down the Web page to see the various image choices.

3. The ***Virtual Reality in Panorama*** will give you a 360-degree panoramic view around the Mars Lander.

4. You can select the ***Lander and Rover on Mars*** to view animation of the landing and the opening of the Lander. It will also simulate moving as the Rover.

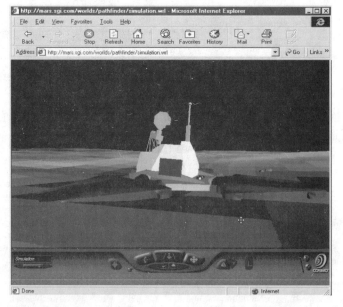

There are several different views of the Virtual Reality Terrain Models. These allow you and your students various views of the landing site, and the locations of the Rover as it traveled over the landing site's surface.

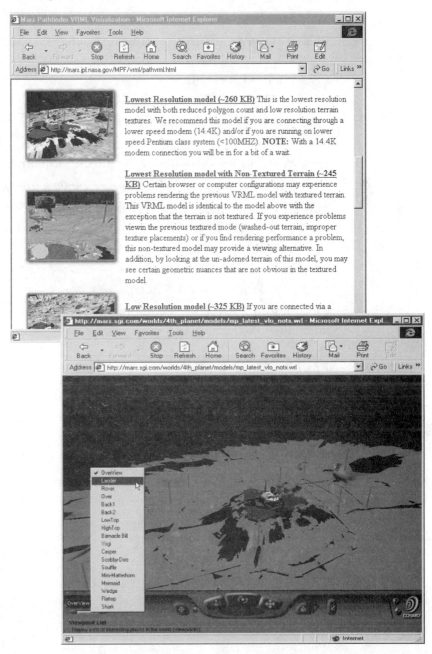

The following sites are additional plug-in programs, and the locations where you can download them.

Chemscape Chime—MDL Information Systems

http://www.mdli.com/download/index.html

Enables viewing of "live" chemical structures.

Crescendo—LiveUpdate

http://www.liveupdate.com

This plug-in allows you to hear MIDI sound files.

HyperStudio Plug-In—Roger Wagner Publishing

http://www.hyperstudio.com/resource/hsplugin/plugin.html

This will allow you to view HyperStudio files which have been published on a Web page.

Shockwave—Macromedia

http://www.macromedia.com/shockwave/

This plug-in lets you view multimedia presentations and interactive Web content.

Flash3—Macromedia

http://www.macromedia.com/software/flash/

This is a viewer for animation and vector graphics.

Acrobat Reader—Adobe

http://www.adobe.com/

This plug-in will allow you to read and to print Portable Document Format (PDF) files.

QuickTime VR—**Apple Computers, Inc.**

http://www.apple.com/quicktime/qtvr/index.html

This is a virtual reality viewer that allows you to view 3-D panoramic movies.

QuickView Plus—**Word Viewer**—**Inso Corporation**

http://www.inso.com/qvp/index.htm

This allows you to view Word documents in your *Internet Explorer* window.

NetView—**Dr. DWG**

http://www.drdwg.com/webviewers/netview/index.html

This plug-in allows you to access and view AutoCAD(r) files in your browser.

VivoActive Player

http://www.vivo.com/products/playfree/vaplayer.html

This allows you to play streaming Vivo movie files.

BrowserWatch

http://browserwatch.internet.com/plug-in.html

This Web site maintains a large list of browser plug-in utilities. You may want to check here if you are trying to find a particular type of plug-in.

Web Browser Plugins—**My Shareware list**

http://www.mysharewarepage.com/plugins.htm

This is another list of plug-in applications that you may want to check.

Helper Applications

A helper application is much like a plug-in program. It is used along with *Internet Explorer* to allow you to view or listen to files you may find on the World Wide Web. Just as there are many plug-in programs, there are many helper application programs available. This section will highlight just a few.

The **Teacher Created Materials** Web site utilizes a helper application.

1. Key this URL into the Address Box and press the ***Enter*** key.

    http://www.teachercreated.com

This will take you to the **Teacher Created Materials** home page.

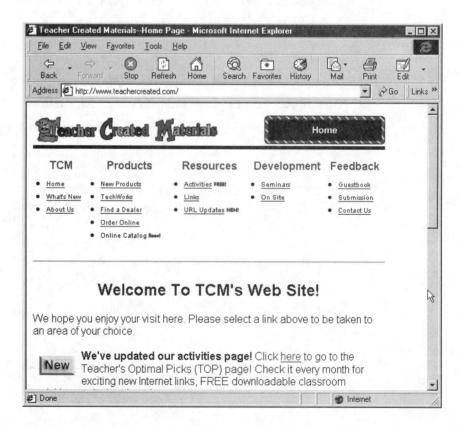

At the top of the screen, you will see a menu of available information.

2. Click the *Activities* hyperlink.

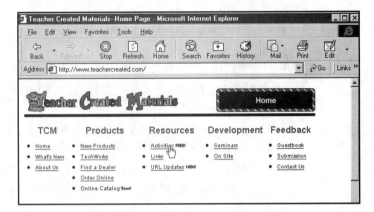

You will see the **Teachers' Optimal Picks** Web page. This has listings of super Web sites you can visit, and it also has links to sample activities from some of their books each month. Visit this page often and download usable worksheets for your classes.

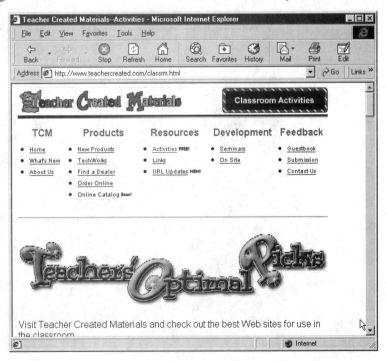

You must have the Adobe *Acrobat Reader* software to read the
PDF (Portable Document Format) files.

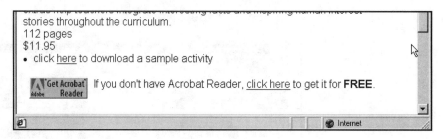

3. If you do not have this software installed on your computer,
   you can click the hyperlink and download it. It is available
   at this URL:

http://www.adobe.com/supportservice/custsupport/download.html

4. Once you have downloaded and installed the *Reader*
   application, you can click the hyperlink for an activity.

The *Reader* works as a plug-in or a helper application. The file
will open in your *Internet Explorer* window.

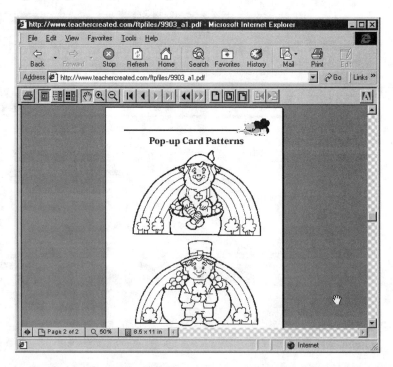

You can also choose to save the PDF file to your computer's hard drive and then view it with the *Adobe Reader*.

5. Right-click the hyperlink and choose **Save Target As** (Windows). Click and hold the hyperlink and choose **Download Link to Disk** (Macintosh).

6. Select a place to save the file. You can then open it more quickly and print pages when you need to.

7. Once you have saved the PDF file, double-click its icon to open it in the *Adobe Reader*.

8. To print the worksheet, click the ***Print*** option in the ***File*** menu of the *Reader* program.

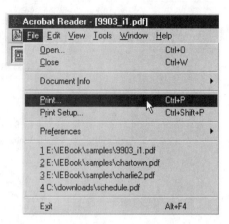

At the bottom of the *Acrobat Reader* window, you can see how many pages are in the document. This document has three pages. You can also see that this view of your document is set at 75% of the regular page size. You can click the size button and increase or decrease as needed.

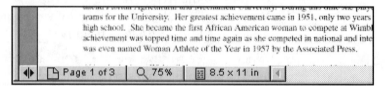

9. To move among the pages, click the arrows at the top of the window.

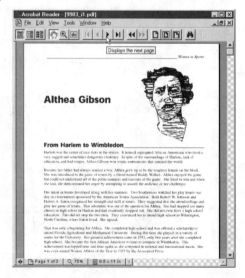

Another Web site that uses the PDF format to offer you a document is the **Kennedy Space Center Shuttle Launch** Web page.

It is located at this URL:

http://www-pao.ksc.nasa.gov/kscpao/schedule/schedule.htm

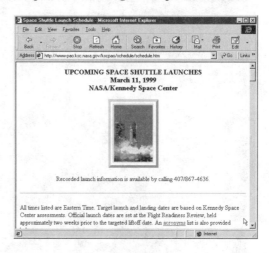

1. Click the hyperlink for the *Launch schedule in table format*.
2. From this site you can print the schedule of shuttle missions for your classroom. It includes the orbiter names, the flight number of that orbiter, the scheduled launch and landing dates, the primary mission, and a list of its crewmembers.

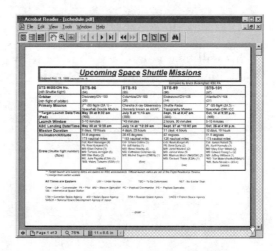

The **Environmental Protection Agency's** Web site has many resources for teachers and students. The **EPA Explorer's Club** is located at the URL:

http://www.epa.gov/kids/

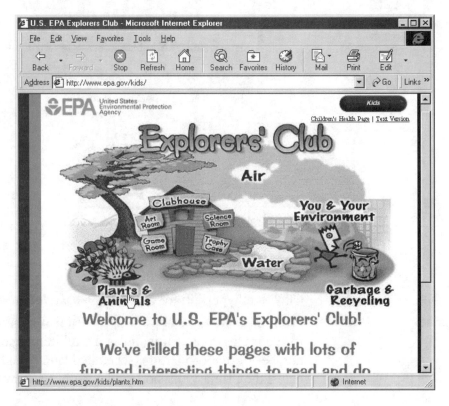

1. Click the graphic hyperlink for ***Plants & Animals***.

This will take you to a Web page for younger students with some activities about plants and animals in the environment.

2. Click the hyperlink to *Charlie Chipmunk*.

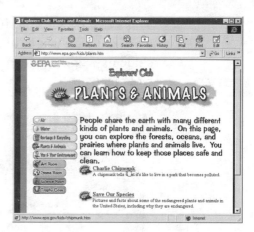

3. Click the hyperlink to download a copy of the coloring book in PDF format.

4. You can right-click the hyperlink and save the coloring book to your hard drive.

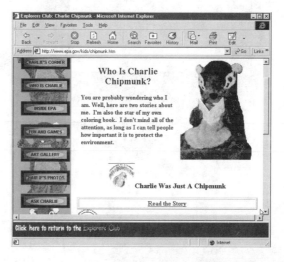

This download will take approximately 50 minutes.

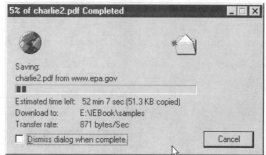

This is a 27-page coloring book about the animals that live in the woods. Once you have saved it, you can print pictures for your students while teaching about the conservation of our parks and woodlands.

There is also a coloring book for teaching students how to stay "lead free" called *Charlie goes to town*.

The **Environmental Protection Agency** also has Web pages and activities for older students. These are located at their **EPA Student Center** Web site.

The site is located at the URL:

http://www.epa.gov/students/

1. Click the different sections of the globe graphic to take you to that part of the Web site.

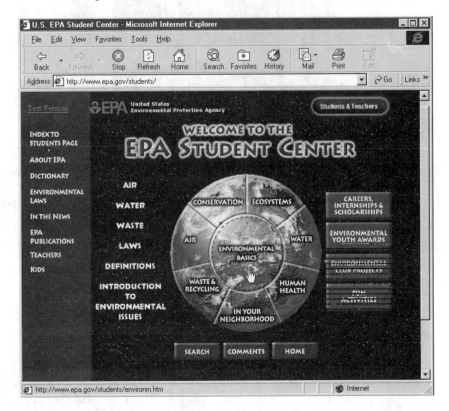

2. For this example, click the center section, ***Environmental Basics***.

3. Click the hyperlink to the *Guide to Environmental Issues*.

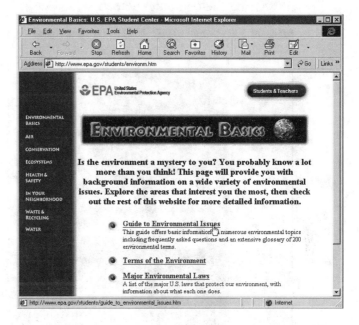

You will be able to download the PDF file for the EPA's guidebook to the most current environmental issues

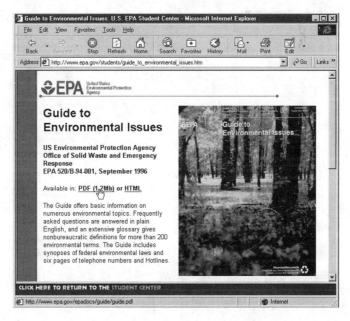

4. Once downloaded, you can either print the guide or read it from the computer screen.

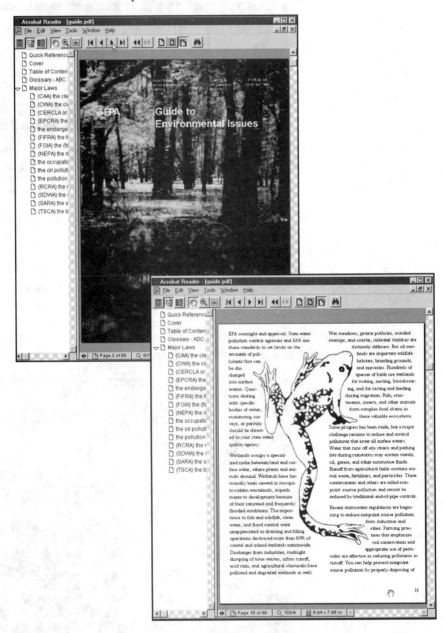

You can move through the pages one at a time or click the topic links in the left-hand portion of the screen.

Another common helper application is the *RealPlayer* audio and video player from *RealNetworks*.

If you do not have this player, you can download the most recent version from their Web site at this URL:

http://www.real.com/

Once you have downloaded and installed the viewer software, you can view streaming movies and hear long audio files without waiting for them to load into your computer's memory. You do not need to save *RealVideo* movies to your hard drive. They play as you access them online.

The **Learning Technologies Channel Archive** from NASA has several movies archived. You can see the following Web pages about the Wright Flyer project at this URL:

http://quest.arc.nasa.gov/ltc/adto/wfo.html

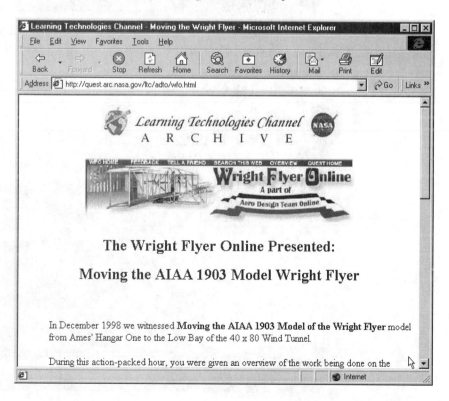

Scroll down the Web page and click the ***RealVideo*** version of the ***Archive of Events***. You will see a video program about moving the model of the Wright flyer to the wind tunnel testing area.

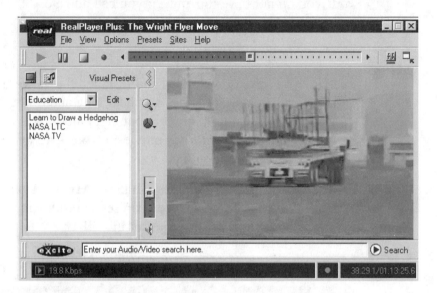

You and your students will view the moving of the full-scale model of the flyer as well as hear a discussion of what will be done with it. There will also be diagrams and small models to illustrate the discussion.

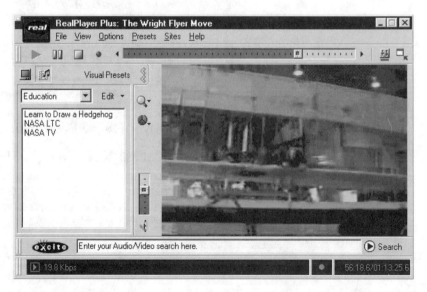

NASA TV is now being broadcast through the **Learning Technologies Channe**l via the *RealPlayer*. Information can be found at this URL:

http://quest.arc.nasa.gov/ltc/live/

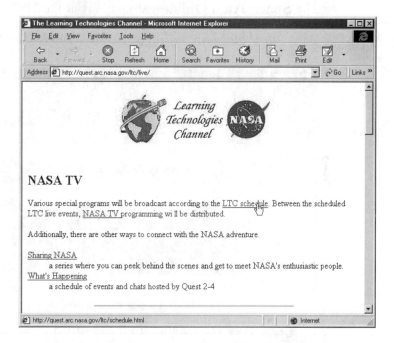

You and your students can view various broadcasts throughout the day. From shuttle launches to views of Earth from space, there is always something worthwhile being broadcast.

The **Learning Technologies Space Team Online** Web site has archived RealVideos of past launches and other space events. These are especially interesting if you and your students have not seen shuttle or rocket launches at night.

The **Space Team Online** Web page is at the URL:

http://quest.arc.nasa.gov/ltc/sto/launch/

The STS-88 launch was at night, and the video will be sure to catch your students' attention.

From its pre-launch position on the launch pad through its ascent into space, the video of the STS-88 launch is breathtaking.

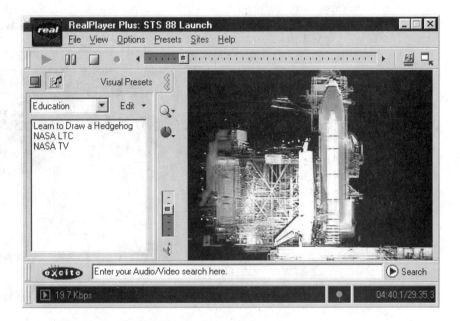

The video is a composite of various camera angles, so you are able to see everything that is happening.

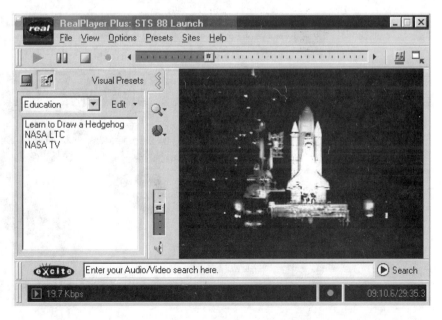

The close-up inset allows you to show your students what is happening during the launch process.

The video follows the shuttle through lift-off with information from ground control, as well.

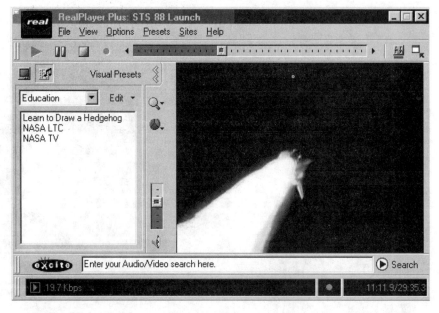

The **NASA Connect** education project uses *RealVideo* movies and animations as a way for you and your students to view the programs.

NASA Connect is located at the URL:

http://edu.larc.nasa.gov/connect/

You may register and participate in the current program or view past activities.

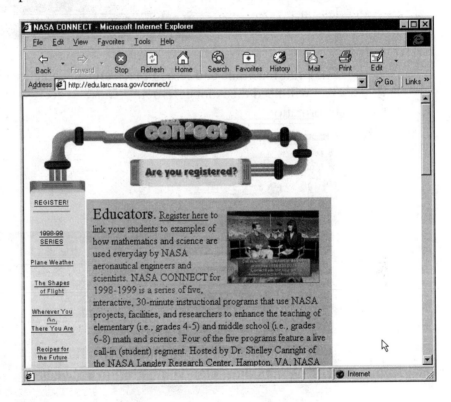

By clicking the video hyperlink, your *RealPlayer* will begin, and you and your students can view the movie or animation that accompanies the lesson.

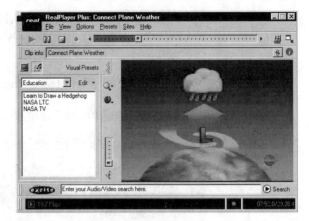

The print materials and lesson plans are available as a PDF file. You will need the Adobe *Acrobat Reader* to access that information.

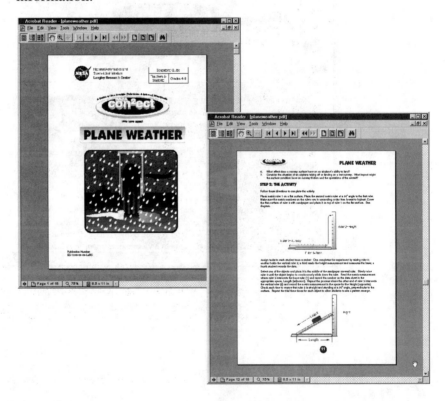

Another site, which has made good use of the *RealVideo* format, is **Jan Brett's Home Page**. Author of such books as *The Hat* and *The Mitten*, her Web site is a terrific place for teachers, parents, and students to visit.

It is located at this URL:

http://www.janbrett.com

Along with lesson ideas, coloring pages, full-page mask graphics, and online postcards, Jan Brett has videotaped directions for drawing Hedgie the Hedgehog.

Scroll down her Web page until you find the hyperlink for *Jan Brett's Videos*. There is one about the book, *The Hat* and also the *Draw a Hedgehog* video.

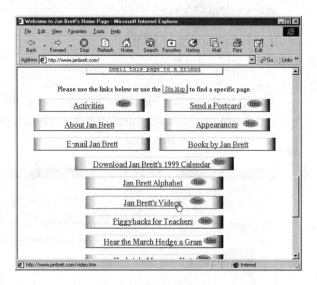

If you have a slower connection, you will need to click the button for *28.8k/56k*.

The video shows Jan Brett demonstrating step-by-step instructions for drawing Hedgie.

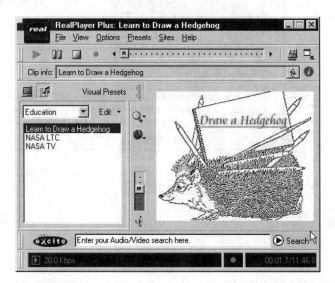

Here are some additional helper applications, and the locations where you can find them.

ACDSee—ACD Systems

http://www.acdsystems.com

Allows viewing of various graphic file formats which your browser does not view. Will also allow file conversion and thumbnail viewing of graphic images in a folder.

LView Pro—MMedia Research Corp.

http://www.lview.com/

This program will help you view, edit, and create many types of graphic files including BMP, PCX, TIFF, JPEG, and GIF files.

Windows Media Player—Microsoft

http://www.microsoft.com/windows/mediaplayer/download/default.asp

Will open and play a large variety of audio and video file formats.

Winzip—Nico Mak Computing, Inc.

http://www.winzip.com/

This application allows you to compress or decompress zipped (PKZIP) files.

Streamworks Player—Xing Technology Corporation

http://www.xingtech.com/downloads/sw/

This helper application plays MPEG audio and video files.

NET TOOB—Digital Bitcasting Corporation

http://www.bitcasting.com/nettoob/

This program plays multimedia files such as MPEG-1, Video for Windows (AVI), *QuickTime* for Windows (MOV), *QuickTime* VR, Autodesk Animations (FLC/FLI), WAV audio and MIDI audio.

MPEG for Real—Digital Bitcasting Corporation

http://www.duplexx.com/welcome.html

This helper application allows you to play MPEG movie files through your RealPlayer.

MidiGate—PRS Corporation

http://www.prs.net/prs/midigate.html

This is a helper application for playing MIDI audio files.

MiniCD, *MiniWAV*, *MiniMedia*, and *MiniTEXT*—The MiniAPPs

http://users.utu.fi/seaavi/minicd.html

These are applications that allow you to view or play a variety of multimedia file formats.

TUCOWS

http://www.tucows.com

This is a repository for shareware programs for Windows and Macintosh. You can search here for new helper applications.

Stroud's Consummate Winsock Applications

http://cws.internet.com/inx.html

This is another Windows application repository.

FilePile

http://filepile.com/nc/start

This is a collection of both Windows and Macintosh shareware files.

Shareware.Com

http://www.shareware.com/

This is another collection of multi-platform shareware where you can search for the latest helper applications.

Searching for Information

Now that you know how to use your browser, how do you find the information you need? There are Web sites with search capabilities to help you do that.

One such site is *Excite*. It offers many services, but we will focus on the search engine. A search "engine" is a search mechanism that not only looks through a listing of Web sites but also searches for keywords and related words within those Web sites. It then returns to you a list of hyperlinks to Web pages that meet your criteria.

It is located at the URL:

http://www.excite.com

The blank search box for the search engine is located at the top right of the Web page. You enter the keywords that you are researching and then click the **Search** button.

1. Key in *Aesop's fables*.
2. Click the **Search** button.

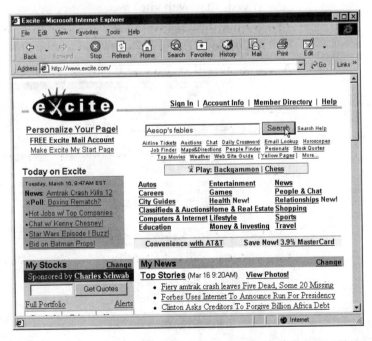

After several seconds, you will see a Web page that has the search's **Web Results**. This is a list of Web sites that are about Aesop, fables, or related topics. The percentage listed is a guide as to how well this Web site matches your search criteria.

3. After reading the short summary, you can click the hyperlink to visit that Web site.

4. Scroll to the bottom of the *Results* page and click the *Next Results* button to see additional Web sites.

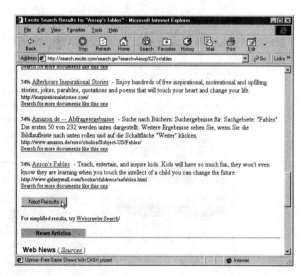

You can add to your search criteria by adding words to the search line. *Excite* offers suggested keywords that you can click to add to your search criteria.

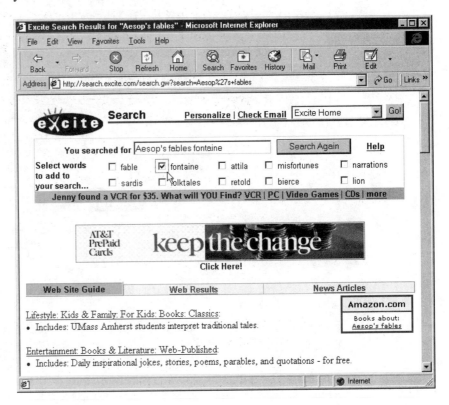

5. Click *fontaine* to add that author to your search for fables or tales.

6. Click the **Search Again** button.

You should see a Web page with suggested Web sites for *Aesop's fables* and stories by Fontaine.

You can also key in additional words of your own.

For additional information about how you can refine your search strategy, check the **Help** page provided by most search engines. *Excite* has a hyperlink to **Help**.

7. Click *Help* to find more information about using *Excite*.

The **Help** page gives you additional information about using the Web site.

The *Search Help* topics give you additional information about what a search is and how to improve your search techniques.

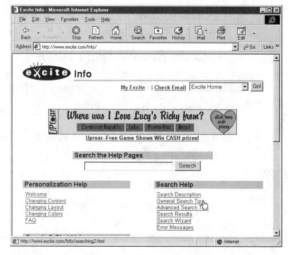

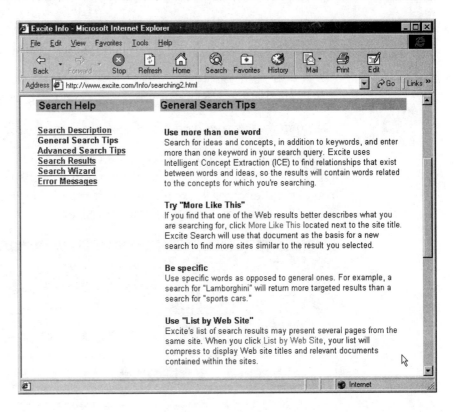

Some of their general search tips apply to other search engines as well. Try using some of these tactics:

- Use more than one word in the search window.
- Click the hyperlink for *Try "More Like This"* to see similar Web pages.
- Use specific words in your search.
- Use quotation marks around phrases to have the search engine look for the entire phrase.
- Use a + sign before words which MUST be in the search results and a - sign before words which you do NOT want to appear.

Another type of search Web site is a categorized list. One of the leading search lists is **Yahoo!**. When you use **Yahoo!**, you are searching through the categories of information.

It is located at the URL:

http://www.yahoo.com

On the main page, you will see a search form blank and a hyperlink for options. You will also see lists of major categories. You can either enter keywords for your search, or you can click one of the categories and follow the divisions.

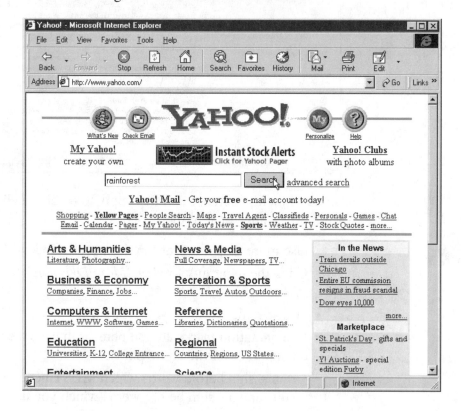

1. Key the word *rainforest* into the search blank.
2. Click the **Search** button.

The search results provide you with additional categories of information and a list of Web site matches.

3. Click the hyperlinks to travel to the Web sites.

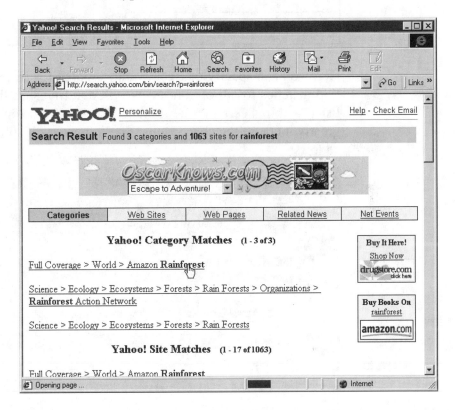

Keep in mind when you are searching, not all of the Web sites that appear in your search results will still be active Web sites. Some Web sites are no longer at the same address, or the server adress may have changed. It can take a while for that information to get to some of the search engines or lists.

4. To improve your search results on **Yahoo!**, click the *advanced search* hyperlink.

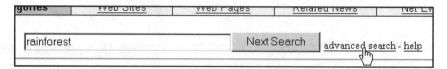

Here you can specify that you want to search for an exact phrase, find matches for all of your keywords, and find sites that were listed within a certain time frame. The time frame option will greatly increase the chances that the Web site will still be an active address.

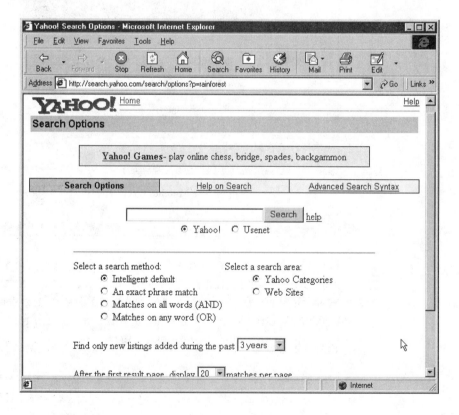

Yahoo! also offers its search capabilities to children. The **Yahooligans!** Web site is a safe place for you and your students to search for information.

It is located at the URL:

http://www.yahooligans.com

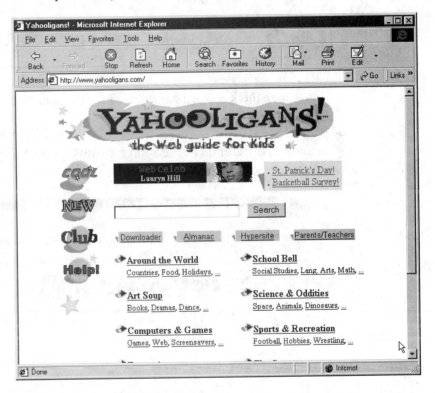

The *Downloader* hyperlink on the main page offers kids graphics, sounds, and video clips to download.

The *Almanac* link takes them to an almanac of facts for kids.

The *Hypersite* link takes kids to an interesting site-of-the-week. There is an explanation of the site and a hyperlink for them to click.

The *Parents/Teachers* hyperlink will lead you to information about teaching with **Yahooligans!** and about teaching search strategies.

The main Web page includes a search blank as well as the category lists.

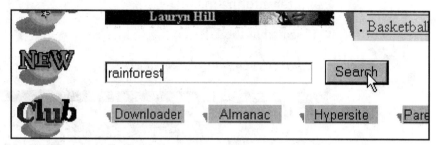

1. Enter the keyword *rainforest* into the search blank.
2. Click the **Search** button.

Notice the difference in the search results. These Web sites are geared toward students and schools.

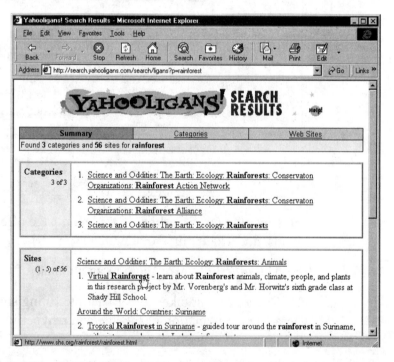

Each Web site listed also has a more lengthy explanation so that your students will be better able to select the Web site most suited to their needs.

If your students are interested in finding information about a listed category of Web sites, they can click the hyperlinks until they find the category they need.

3. Click the ***Around the World*** hyperlink.

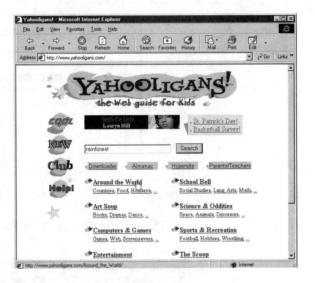

The next Web page is a list of categories the number of Web sites in each category. ***Around the World*** leads you to categories such as Archeology, Cultures, Flags, Languages, and Travel.

Another search Web site for students is the **Ask Jeeves for Kids!** site. This site lets kids ask questions about a variety of topics.

It is located at the URL:

http://www.ajkids.com/

In order to search for information, enter a question into the search blank and click the *Ask* button.

The response Web page will provide other leading questions to narrow the search criteria. Students can select the link that best fits their question.

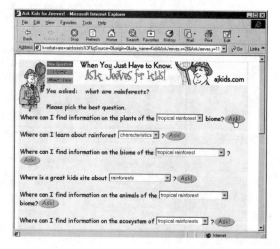

Clicking one of the questions will lead students to a Web page about that topic. These Web pages are from a variety of resources.

At the bottom of the response Web page, students will find the results from searches by several other search engines. These Web sites have been approved through the online filter, *Surf-Watch*. Students can click a drop-down menu and choose from the recommended Web sites.

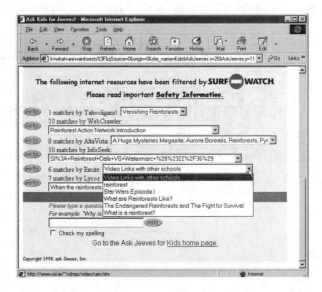

The leading questions are different depending on the initial topic. The resource Web sites offer a quick way for students to find information about their questions.

The **Ask Jeeves for Kids!** Web site also offers teacher and student resources. By clicking the buttons for ***Teacher*** or ***Student***, you can access other sites that have been picked out by Jeeves.

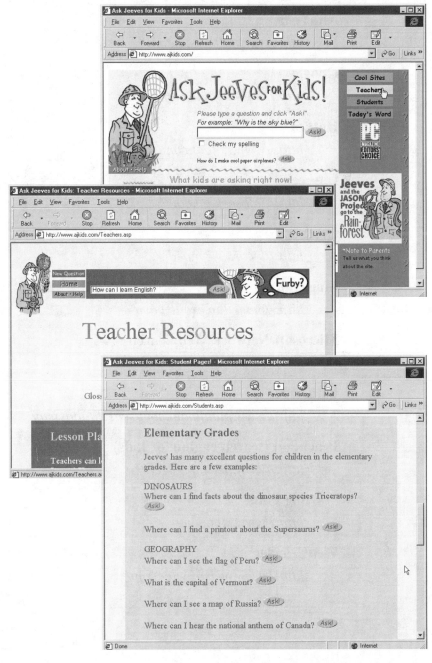

There are many search engines and lists online. Different lists sometimes have different Web pages listed. Here are the URLs of some you may want to try.

AltaVista
http://www.altavista.com/

Google
http://www.google.com/

HotBot
http://www.hotbot.com/

Infoseek
http://infoseek.go.com/

Lycos
http://lycos.cs.cmu.edu/

Magellan
http://magellan.excite.com/

Microsoft Network Web Search
http://search.msn.com/

Pathfinder
http://www.pathfinder.com/search/altavista/

PeachPod (search engine for kids)
http://www.peachpod.com/

Starting Point
http://www.stpt.com/

WebCrawler
http://www.webcrawler.com/

Using Online Forms

As you visit various Web sites on the World Wide Web, you will encounter some that ask you to fill in blanks and submit information. A good rule is to be wary of what sites are asking for what information. You should also instruct your students never to fill out forms with their personal information such as name, address, or phone number.

There will be times, however, when you want to subscribe to a mailing list, order software or merchandise, or enter data into a project Web site.

The **Landmark Project** Web site has a wonderful project that was started back in 1987. It is called the Global Grocery List.

The **Landmark Project** site is at this URL:

http://www.landmark-project.com/home.html

Landmarks for Schools Web site is at:

http://www.landmark-project.com/

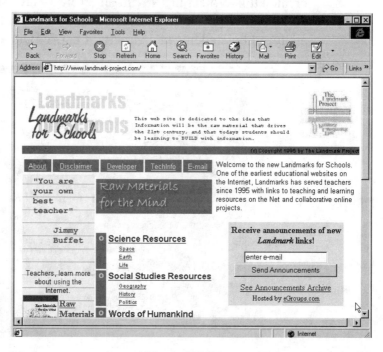

To access the Global Grocery List project, scroll to the bottom of the Web page and click the hyperlink.

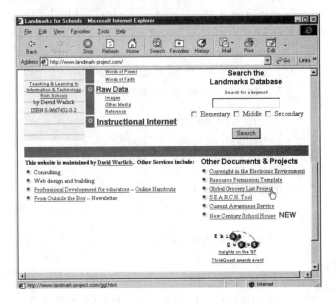

David Warlick, the creator of **The Landmark Project** Web site, created this project in 1987 in an effort to have students collaborate over the Internet and share real data that could be analyzed by students in a variety of curriculum areas.

Your students collect data about local grocery prices. They enter this information into the main database from the Web site. They can then retrieve data from many cities and countries to compare/contrast food prices. Your students should be able to draw some conclusions about agriculture and marketing based on some of the prices.

You can choose to view the prices of some or all of the data. The search can be limited to a specific year and a maximum number of records per reply.

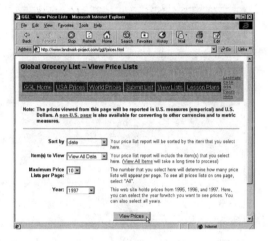

The reply to your query is organized according to location. The prices are set in columns so that you and your students can easily read them.

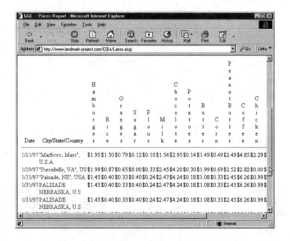

To submit your information, have your students find the prices of the items on the grocery list for your location. You may want to average prices from different stores to get a class price. You then must enter the data into the database. This is done through a form located on the Web site.

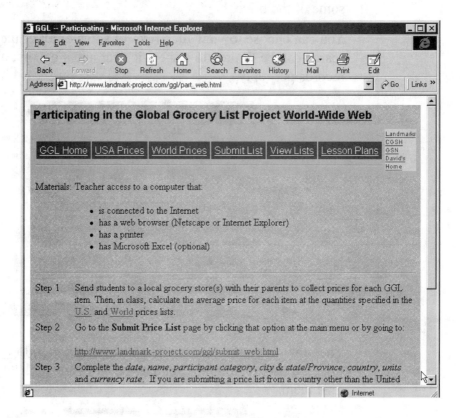

1. Click the hyperlink to go to the *Submit Price* Web page.

2. Students should enter data about their location and when they collected their prices.

3. Use the Tab key to move from blank to blank within the form.

4. Scroll down the page and enter all of the prices.

5. When students are finished entering the prices, click the ***Submit Your Price List*** button.

In addition to the Global Grocery List, the **Landmark Project** Web site has many resources for teachers and students.

Select a heading on the **Landmarks for Schools** Web page, and you will find resources for integrating Web sites into your curriculum.

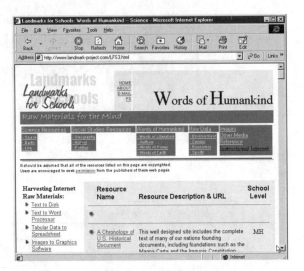

The **New Century School House** is a project that allows teachers to share their ideas and dreams about what schools in the future should be like. Visit some of the rooms in the schoolhouse or "occupy" a room that you have created with your own ideas.

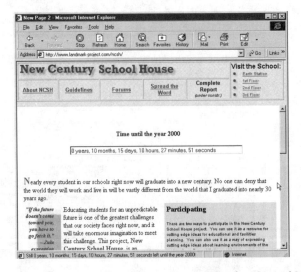

WebCams—Your Window to the World

There are many sites on the Web that have automatically reloading camera images of various objects or locations. These are called "webcams." They are software-run cameras that take a picture at a designated interval of time. The software then uploads the image to a Web page.

You do not need any special software or plug-ins to view webcam images. They will appear in the associated Web page window. Some of the Web pages will automatically reload so that you see the new image with each picture taken. On other pages, you will have to click your *Refresh* button to view the newest image.

The following are some examples of webcams you and your students can visit.

The **Washington State Department of Transportation** has a Web site that has image maps with markers that show various webcams along the freeways of the Puget Sound area.

The Web site is located at this URL:

http://www.wsdot.wa.gov/regions/northwest/NWFLOW/camera/

Click the buttons to switch views from Seattle to Tacoma.

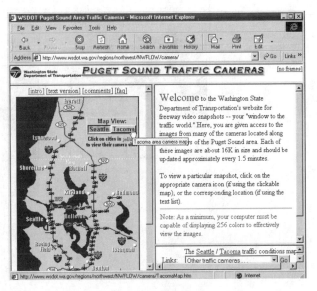

Click the camera graphics on the image map to see the different camera views.

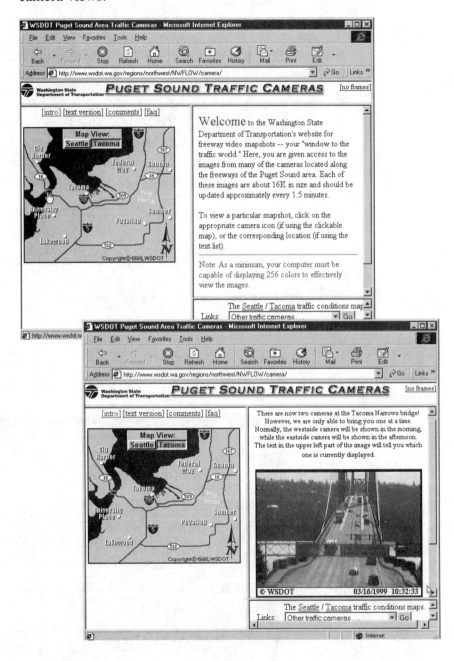

The **National Weather Service** in Grand Junction, Colorado maintains a webcam with an image from the top of Grand Mesa.

http://www.crh.noaa.gov/gjt/index.html

Scroll down the page and click the ***Weather Camera*** hyperlink.

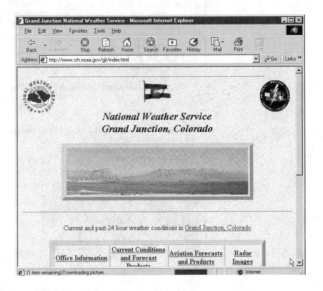

Webcams such as this one are great tools for showing weather differences in various parts of the country and around the world.

The **US Geological Survey** maintains a webcam at the Streamflow-Gaging Station along the Verde River.

http://www.daztcn.wr.usgs.gov/webcam/cam_09511300.html

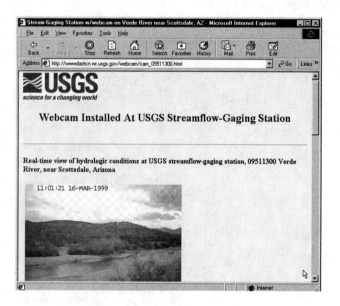

Scroll down the Web page to read additional information about the equipment used and how the project was set up.

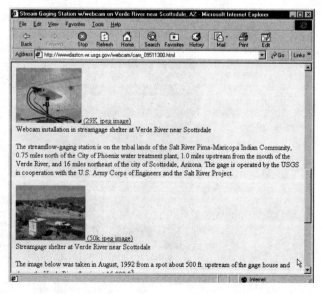

NASA Kennedy Space Center maintains a Web page with a dozen webcams from various sites. You can watch shuttle and rocket launches, view weather conditions in the area, and see work being completed in the Space Station Processing Facility.

http://www.ksc.nasa.gov/shuttle/countdown/video/

By clicking the hyperlinks, you can find additional information about each of the video feeds such as the Stardust rocket mission.

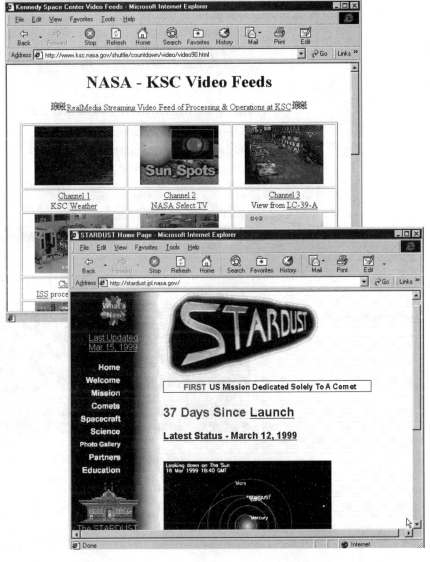

The **Project Galileo** Web site also has reloading images. They are simulated views of the Galileo spacecraft. They are computer generated and are reloaded every five minutes.

http://www.jpl.nasa.gov/galileo/countdown/:://www.jpl.nasa.gov/galileo/countdown/

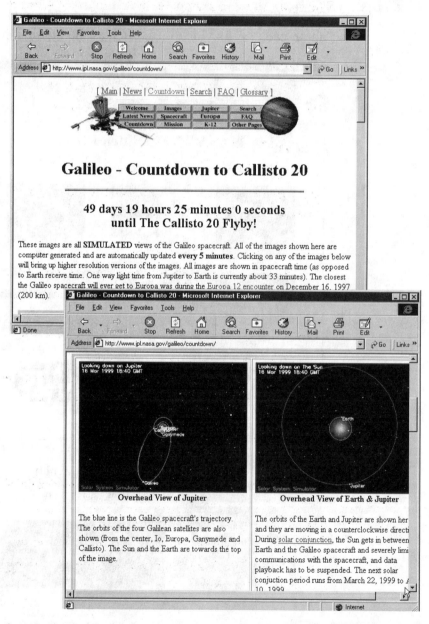

Here are some more Web sites where you can find additional webcams or information about creating one for your classroom.

EarthCam

http://www.earthcam.net/

This Web site is a searchable index to many webcams around the world.

The WebCam Resource

http://www.webcamresource.com/Regional/

This is another searchable index of webcams.

WebCam World

http://www.webcamworld.com/

This site contains information about webcams, new webcams online, and a searchable index.

North American WebCams

http://gallery.uunet.be/internetpress/star00.htm

This site contains a list of webcams in North America.

Coastal Imaging Lab—Oregon State University

http://cil-www.oce.orst.edu:8080/

This site maintains webcams along various coastlines. Click the menu list or the image map to see the webcams.

Webcam32—Neil Kolban

http://kolban.com/webcam32/

This site has Windows '95+ software to manage a webcam.

SiteCam—Rearden Technology

http://www.rearden.com/sitecam/default.html

This site has Macintosh software to support sending webcam images to a Web site.

Microsoft *Outlook Express*

Outlook Express is the electronic mail (e-mail) component of the Microsoft *Internet Explorer* package. You will use this utility to exchange e-mail with other Internet users.

You can open the *Outlook Express* program by clicking the **Mail** button on the toolbar in *Internet Explorer*.

 You can also open *Outlook Express* by double-clicking the icon on your desktop or in a folder.

You will see this splash screen graphic as *Outlook Express* is loading.

Account Setup

To set up your account information, follow the directions, and use your Internet access account (Windows). Accounts can be set up by choosing *Preferences* from the Edit menu and choosing *Email* (Macintosh).

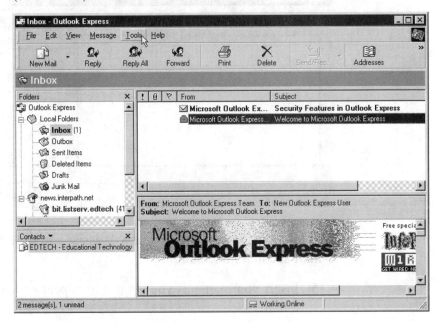

1. Click *Tools*.
2. Select *Accounts* from the *Tools* drop-down menu.

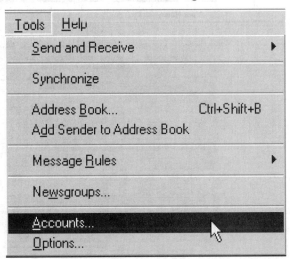

You will see this dialog box.

3. Select the *Mail* tab and click the *Add* button.
4. Select *Mail* from the drop-down menu.

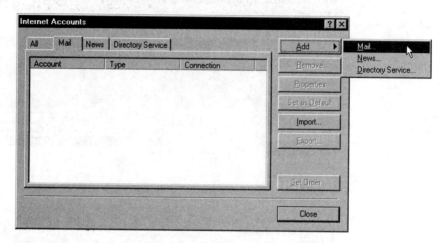

The Internet Connection Wizard will assist you in setting up your e-mail account information.

5. Insert your name as you want it to appear on your out-going e-mail.
6. Click the *Next* button to continue to the next step.

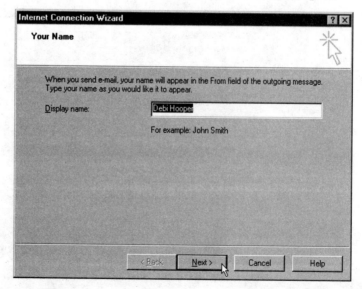

7. Enter the e-mail address you want others to use as your return address to reply to your messages.

8. Click the *Next* button to continue.

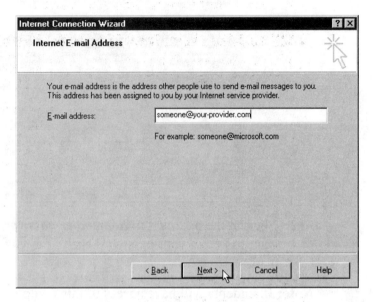

9. Enter the incoming and outgoing server information from your Internet Service Provider.

10. Click the *Next* button to continue.

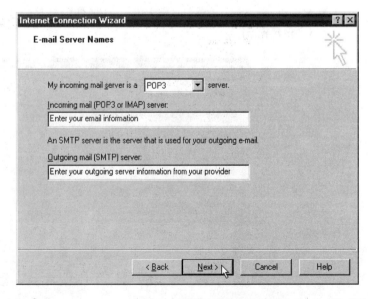

11. Key in your *Account name* and *Password*.

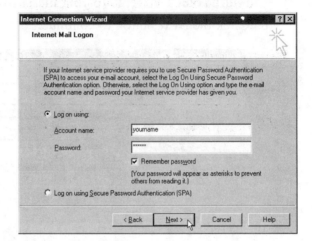

12. Click in the box next to *Remember password* if you do not want to key in your password each time you check your e-mail.

Note: If students will have access to this computer, you may not want to keep your password on file. This would prohibit them from being able to check your new e-mail messages.

13. Click the *Next* button to continue.

You have now completed setting up *Outlook Express* for checking your e-mail.

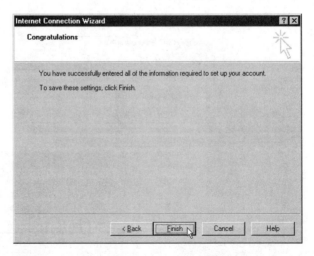

14. Click the ***Finish*** button if you think all of the information is correct. You can edit the information later if it is incorrect or if it changes.

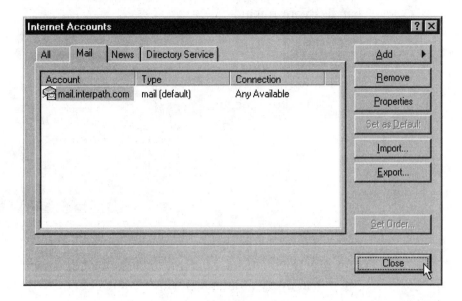

You can set up additional e-mail accounts, if you have more than one. Once you are finished setting up all of your accounts, click the ***Close*** button to return to *Outlook Express*.

You can also use this dialog box to delete e-mail account information if your service provider or e-mail addresses change.

Setting Options

Once you have your account set up, you can set your program options. These options help you personalize how *Outlook Express* handles your e-mail.

1. Click *Tools*.
2. Select *Options* from the drop-down menu.

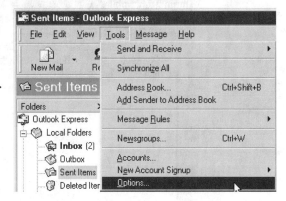

The *General* tab has some simple choices you can make.

You may decide to set *Outlook Express* to check your e-mail more often than every 30 minutes which is the default setting.

You can set it to check your e-mail every 10 minutes in order to keep your Internet connection active if your provider automatically logs you off after 15 minutes of inactive time. This will help keep the computer online for groups of students who may be rotating through a computer station set up in your classroom.

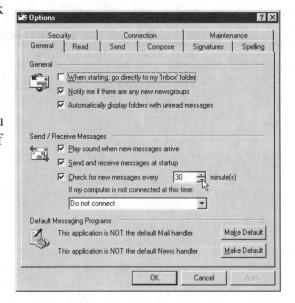

3. Click the **Read** tab to see the options.

The **Read** tab provides options for reading your incoming e-mail.

You will most likely want to keep the original settings.

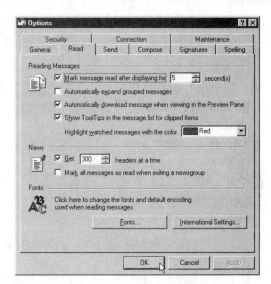

4. Click the **Send** tab to view those options.

You will most likely want to keep the **Send** options as they appear.

You can change the **Mail Sending Format** to **Plain Text** if you are not sure if your recipients can read HTML formatted messages.

Note: Definitely change to **Plain Text** format if you are submitting messages to any mail lists.

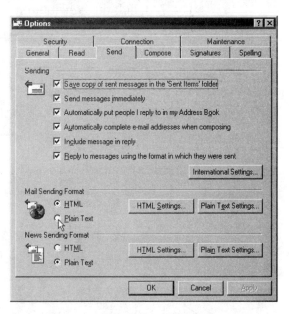

5. Click the **Compose** tab to view the options.

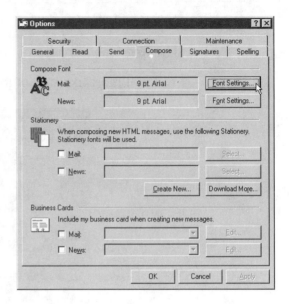

Here you can change the font style and size for composing e-mail messages.

This is important if you have younger students composing e-mail messages. You can set it to a large font size so that they can key in their own messages easily.

6. Click the **Signatures** tab to set up a signature file.

If you want a standard signature paragraph attached to each e-mail message you send, you can enter it here. You can create more than one signature.

7. Click the **New** button to create a signature.

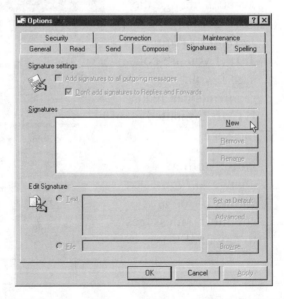

The Signature #1 line will be automatically added.

8. You will then enter the signature in the Text blank.

If you are using this at school, you can enter information such as your school's address and Web page address.

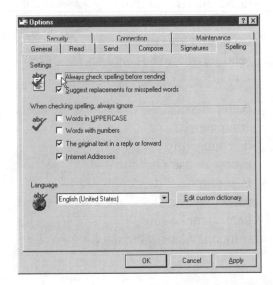

9. Click the **Apply** button to set this as a signature. This will be the default (or normally used) signature. You can set additional signatures from which to choose when sending messages.

10. Click the **Spelling** tab to set those options.

You can check the box next to **Always check spelling before sending**. This is a good way to make sure your students check the spelling in their e-mail messages before sending them.

11. Click the **Security** tab to view the options here.

If you choose to select a more restricted security level, *Outlook Express* will use the security level you have set up in *Internet Explorer*.

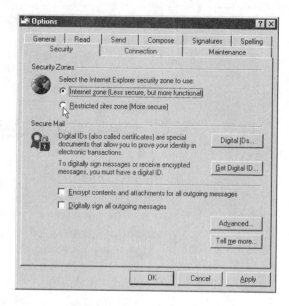

12. Click the **Connection** tab to set those options.

You will most likely want to keep these settings as they appear. *Outlook Express* will then double-check with you before you switch Internet connections.

If you will be using your connection for browsing or other applications, you will not want to disconnect each time you finish sending and receiving e-mail.

Note: If your computer is disconnecting each time you use *Outlook Express* to send or receive mail, check here to make sure someone has not changed this setting.

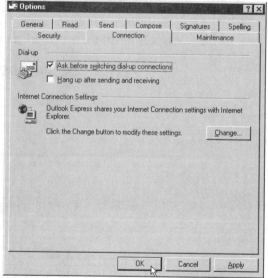

13. Click the *Maintenance* tab to set the options.

To save space on your hard drive, you can choose to set *Outlook Express* to automatically empty the messages you have moved to the *Deleted Items* folder.

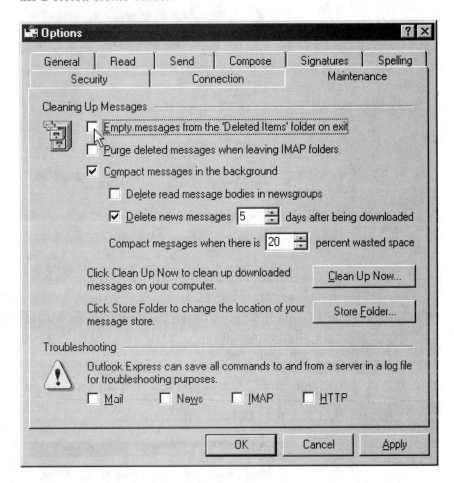

If you want to set up a special folder on your hard drive for storing e-mail messages, you can click the *Store Folder* button and designate a new folder location.

Receiving and Sending E-mail

When you first open *Outlook Express*, you will see this screen.

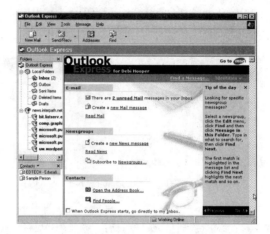

1. Click the ***Send/Receive*** button to get new e-mail messages.

2. If you chose not to save your account password when you set up that information, you will need to enter your password when prompted.

It will appear as **** as you key it in for security purposes.

3. Click the ***OK*** button to continue.

You will see a dialog box as your computer connects with your Internet provider and downloads any e-mail messages you may have.

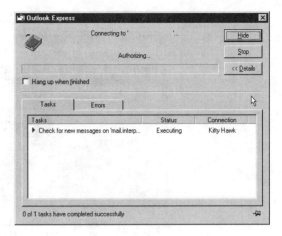

4. Click **Inbox**. Your new e-mail messages will appear in the upper right-hand box.

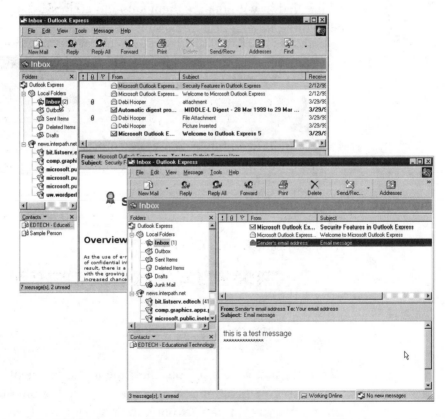

5. Click the e-mail heading, and the message will appear in the lower box.

6. If this is an e-mail message from someone that you want to answer, click the **Reply** button.

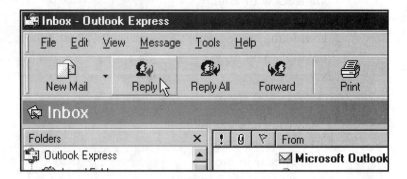

The e-mail composition window opens automatically. The **To:** line is filled in with the recipient's e-mail address. The **Subject:** line is filled in with "Re: their subject line."

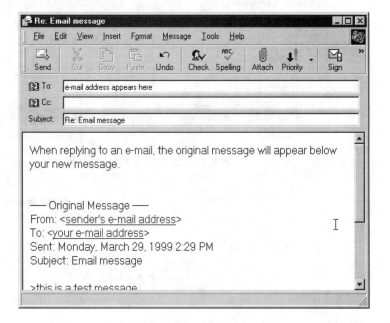

7. You can now key in your message to the recipient. Their message will automatically appear at the bottom of your reply. You can move your cursor down the screen and delete a portion of or their entire message. This is helpful if you want to retain part of their message within your reply.

8. When you have finished writing your reply, click the **Send** button on the Composition window tool bar to send the e-mail message.

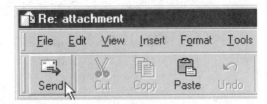

You will also want to write new messages to people whose e-mail addresses you have.

1. Click the **New Mail** button on the *Outlook Express* tool bar. The Composition window will open.

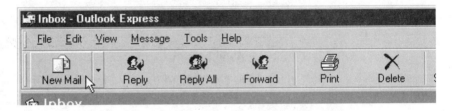

2. Enter the recipient's e-mail address in the **To:** line.

3. Enter a subject heading in the **Subject:** blank.

4. Type your message in the body space.

5. Click the **Send** button when you have completed your message.

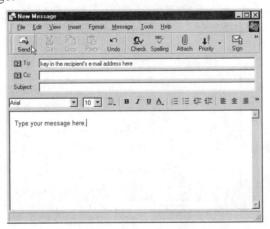

Address Book

You can keep a directory of e-mail addresses in the Address Book. You will not have to scroll through all of your e-mail messages to find someone's address.

1. Select *Address Book* from the *Tools* menu.

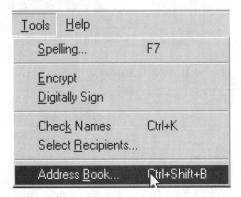

2. Click the *New* button.
3. Select *New Contact* to create a new entry in your address book.

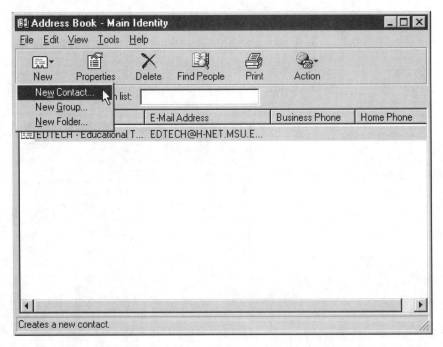

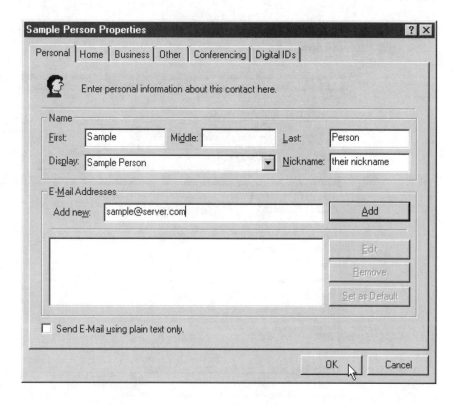

4. Enter the information about this person. You can fill in as little or as much information as you want, but you must fill in an e-mail address and name.

5. Once you have completed entering information, click the *OK* button to return to the Address Book window.

You will now see your address entry listed in your Address Book window.

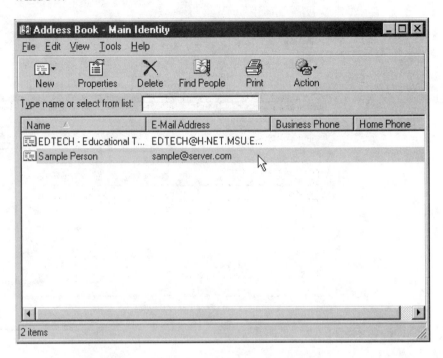

6. When you are finished adding addresses, you can close the Address Book by clicking the *X* in the upper right-hand corner or selecting ***Exit*** from the ***File*** menu.

7. To send an e-mail message to someone in your Address Book, click the ***To:*** button next to the e-mail address blank.

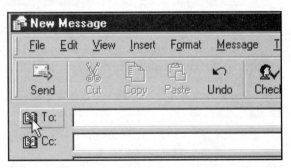

Your Address Book entries will appear in the left-hand window of the *Select Recipients* dialog box.

8. Select a recipient's name in the list.

9. Click the *To:* button in the center of the dialog box to add this recipient to the list on the right-hand side.

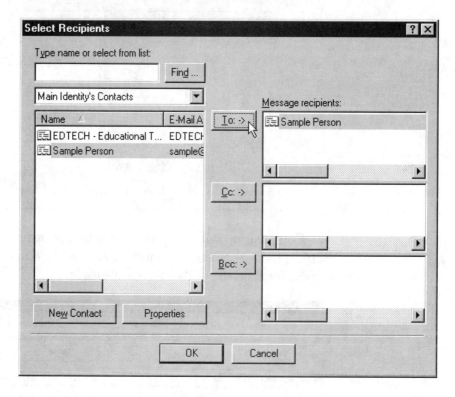

You can select as many recipients for a single e-mail message as you need. By clicking the *Cc:* button, you can select one main recipient and also select several others to send "carbon copies."

The *Bcc:* button works as a "blind carbon copy" option. You will send e-mail messages to multiple recipients but their e-mail addresses will not appear in the *From:* region of the e-mail.

10. Once you have selected all of the recipients, click the **OK** button to continue.

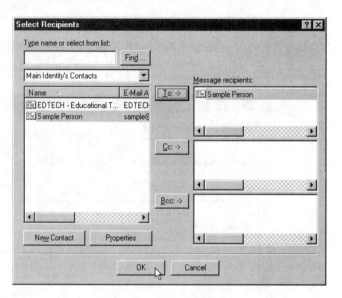

The Composition window will automatically open. The Address Book entry will be entered into the **To:** line. You simply enter a subject line and the body of your message.

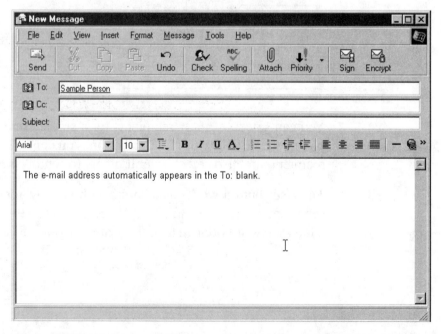

Inserting Files in an E-mail Message

You can send other documents, graphics, or program files with an e-mail message.

Keep in mind that the recipient must have a program to view or read whatever file you send. You must be aware that large files will take some time to process through your e-mail server as well as that of the recipient.

1. Select *File Attachment* from the *Insert* menu.

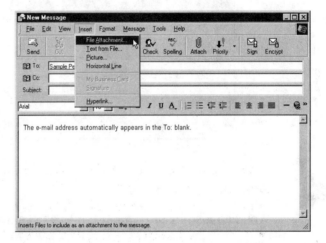

2. Find the file you want to send and select it by clicking it.
3. Click the *Attach* button.

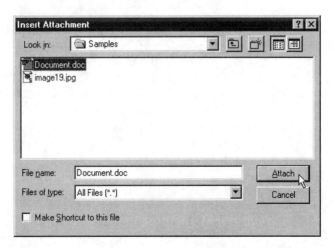

You will see the file listed in the ***Attach:*** blank. You can send more than one file attachment with a single e-mail message.

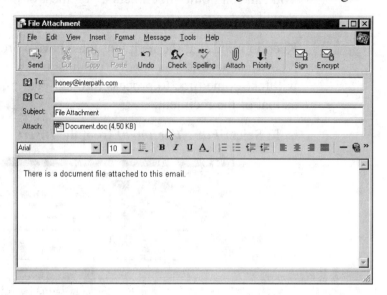

 Note: Again, be aware of the collective size of the files you are sending.

You can also insert a picture into an e-mail message.

1. Select ***Picture*** from the ***Insert*** menu.

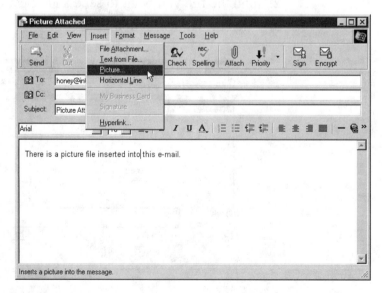

2. Click the ***Browse*** button to look for the picture file.

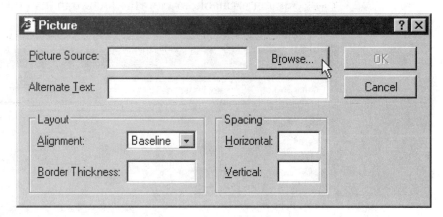

3. Select the picture file you want to attach.
4. Click the ***Open*** button.

5. Enter *Alternate Text* to describe the picture in case the recipient is unable to view the picture in his e-mail program.

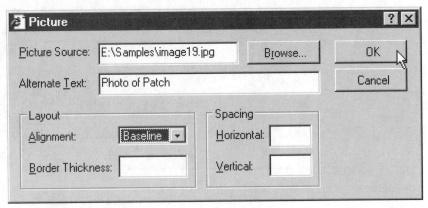

6. Click the *OK* button to continue.
7. Click the *Send* button to send your message with the picture inserted.

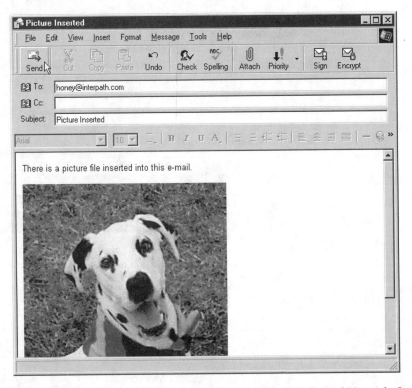

Receiving E-mail with a File Inserted

What do you do when you get an e-mail message with a file inserted? The list of received e-mail will show a paper clip graphic to let you know there is a file inserted or attached.

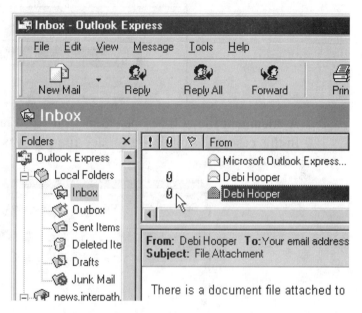

1. Click that e-mail header to open it.
2. Click the large paper clip button located on the right side of the of the e-mail message heading.

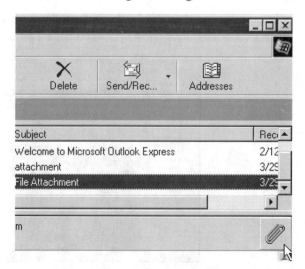

You will see a drop-down menu with a list of the attached files and a choice to *Save Attachments*.

3. Click the attachment listing to view it in the appropriate software.

A document file will be opened in your word processing program. In this case, the sample was a .doc file and was opened in *Microsoft Word*.

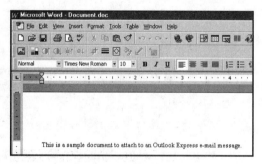

If a picture is inserted into the e-mail message, it will automatically appear in the body of the e-mail.

Checking Your Spelling

Outlook Express has a spelling checker utility that you can use to make sure you have not made a spelling or typing error in your e-mail messages.

In the following message, the word typed has been misspelled on purpose.

1. To start to spell check your message, click the *Spelling* button on the New Message tool bar.

The *Spelling* dialog box will appear. It will find the first incorrectly spelled word and suggest possible spelling choices.

2. Select the correct spelling.

3. Click the *Change* button.

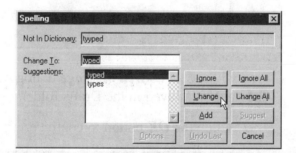

4. Once the spelling check is completed, simply click the *OK* button to send your e-mail message.

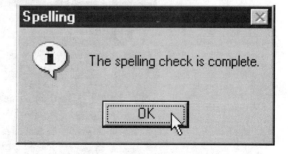

Saving a Draft of an E-mail Message

There may be times when you are working on an e-mail message and need to stop to do something else. You can save the draft, reopen it, and finish it at a later time

1. Select *Save* from the *File* drop-down menu.

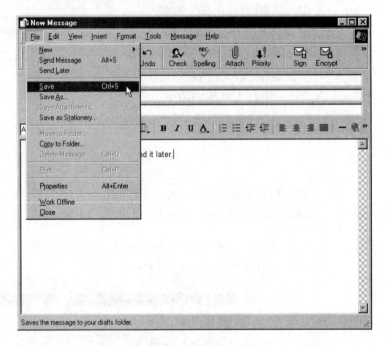

You will see this *Saved Message* dialog box. It tells you that your message was saved in the Drafts folder.

2. Click the *OK* button to continue.

3. When you are ready to work on the e-mail message again, you can find it in the Drafts folder.

4. Double-click the message header to open the Composition window again.

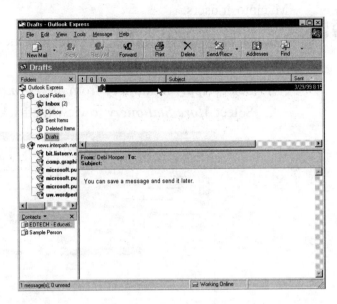

Once you have re-opened the e-mail message, you can add to it and then send it as usual.

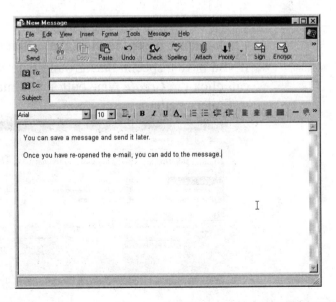

Using Stationery

To "dress up" your e-mail message, add stationery patterns. You need to be sure that your recipient can view HTML formatted e-mail before you send the message. Stationery is not available for Macintosh users.

Note: Make sure you only send plain text messages to mailing lists.

1. Select *Apply Stationery* from the *Format* menu.
2. Select *More Stationery* to view the background designs.

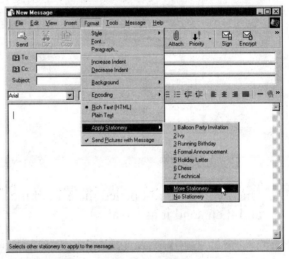

3. Click the file names to view the different stationery designs.
4. If you have a special background pattern that you like, you can click the *Create New* button and make your own stationery pattern.

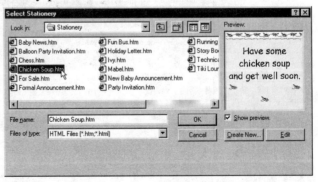

Once you have selected a stationery design, you will see it in the composition window.

You can also change your font style and size to create a special message to send to the recipient.

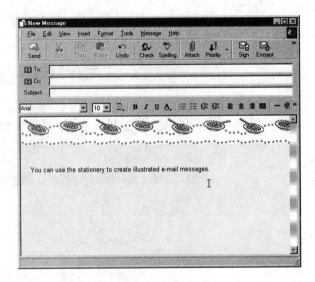

You can also create a special message by adding a simple color for your background.

Select *Color* from the *Background* choices on the *Format* menu.

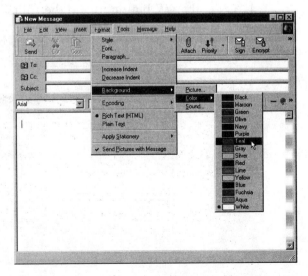

Organizing Your E-mail

To bring some order to your e-mail instead of saving it all in your Inbox, you can create additional mail folders and move related messages into them.

1. Select *Folder* from the *File* drop-down menu.
2. Select *New* from the *Folder* menu.

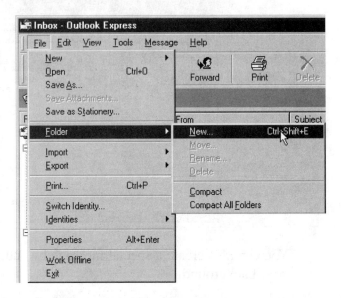

3. Enter a name for the new mail folder.
4. Click the *OK* button to add the folder to your list.

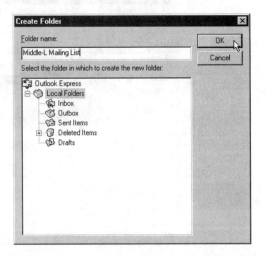

The new mailbox will appear in the list in the left-hand box.

5. To move a message into that mailbox, click the message you want to move. Do not release your mouse button, but drag the message over to the correct folder in your list.

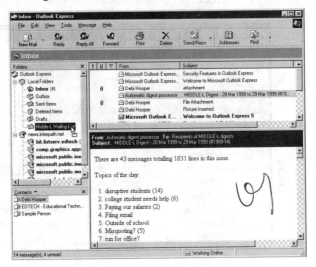

6. Release the mouse button when the cursor is over the highlited folder listing.

7. To see messages in a folder, click the folder name. Messages will now appear in the list on the right-hand side.

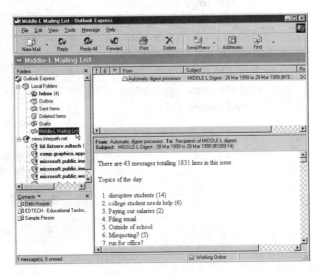

Deleting E-mail Messages

You probably will not want to keep every e-mail message you receive. You will want to delete some periodically.

1. Select the e-mail message you want to delete.

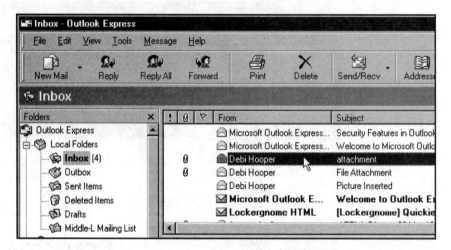

2. Right-click the message you want to delete.

3. Click the *Delete Message* option from the drop-down menu.

This will not permanently delete the message. It will move the message to the *Deleted Items* folder.

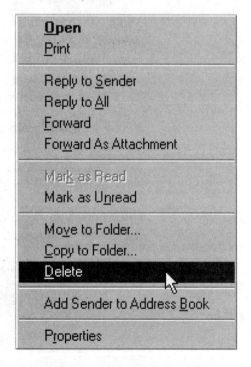

4. Click the ***Deleted Messages*** folder icon to open that folder. You will then see a list of all of the messages you have sent to that folder.

5. To permanently delete a message, select it, right-click the message, and select the ***Delete Message*** option or press the ***Delete*** key on your keyboard.

6. You will be asked to confirm this action. Click the ***Yes*** button if you are sure you want to delete the message.

Once messages have been deleted from the Deleted Messages folder, they have been removed from your computer.

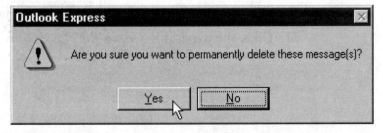

E-mail in the Classroom

Now that you have the ability to send and receive e-mail messages, how do you incorporate that into the curriculum? There are many Web sites that have ideas for using e-mail as part of a classroom activity.

One site is **ePals**. It is located at this URL:

http://www.epals.com/

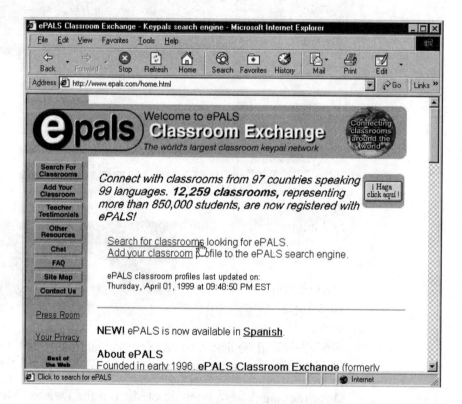

You can search through their database of classrooms from all over the world to find partners for collaborative projects.

1. Click the hyperlink *Search for classrooms*.

The newest additions to the project's list will be located at the bottom of this page.

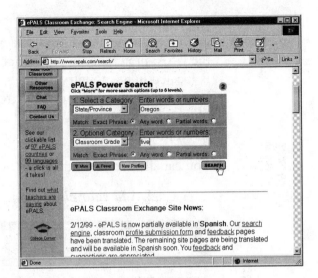

You can also find **ePals** by searching various criteria.

2. Fill in the form with your selections for age, grade, location, etc.

3. Click the *Search* button.

Projects are listed with teacher name, languages, e-mail address, grade levels, student ages, number of students per class, location, and a description of their project.

Here are a few sample project descriptions:

Description: We are currently studying weather and will be studying recycling beginning in April. We would like to communicate with any class that would be interested in sharing information with us on these topics as well as communicating with us in general. I will be using this experience not only as a lesson in technology but in writing, too. We would like to correspond about 1x per week.

Description: I am looking for native Spanish speakers, anywhere in the world, that would like to communicate via e-mail with some of my students. I teach levels 2 and 3. I would like the communication to alternate languages; one time in English and the next time in Spanish. That way both groups can practice their second language. We are flexible with subject areas, frequency, length, etc.

Description: I have 27 students, 9 boys and 18 girls. I am interested in matching each student with a keypal somewhere in the USA, preferably in another corner of the country. Our school is located in the country, although it is only 20 miles from Portland, Oregon and 10 miles from the nearest suburb. I would like to correspond with a class that lives in the inner city or a very small town.

You can also create and submit your own project idea.

1. Click *Add your classroom*.

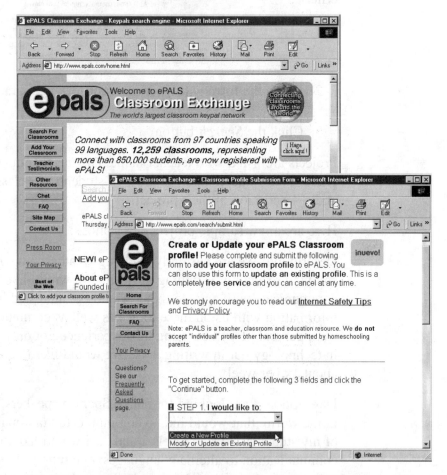

2. Fill out the form to add your class profile and a new project.

You can return to this Web page later to modify your project ideas.

3. Fill in all of the information about your class and include a description of your project.

Note: You might want to participate in a few projects before starting one of your own. Read through several others before creating your own description.

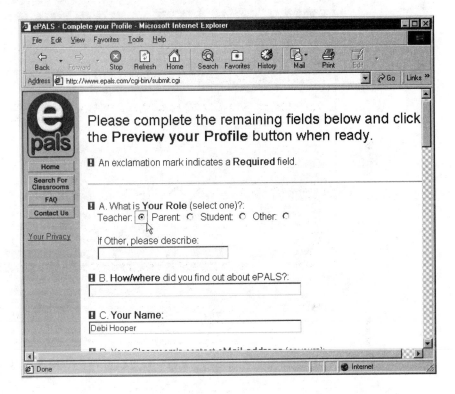

Make sure you practice sending and receiving e-mail before participating in one of these projects. It is important to make sure that everyone has a successful experience with the collaboration.

The **Global Schoolhouse** maintains a large database of online projects. They are located at this URL:

http://www.gsn.org/

1. Click the *Projects* button to see current activities.

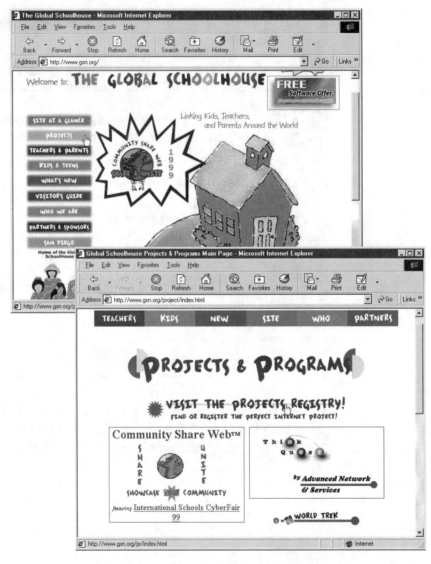

2. Click the banner to go to the *Projects Registry*. This is where you can search for projects that meet your criteria.

The **Global Schoolhouse** maintains a registry of current projects as well as an archive of past projects.

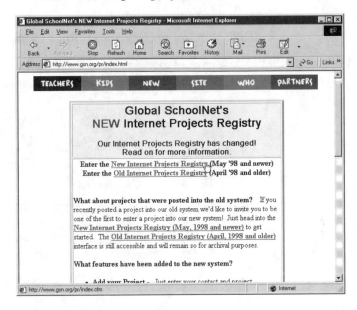

3. Click *Simple Project Search* to find projects.
4. Click *Advanced Project Search* to find projects that meet selected criteria.

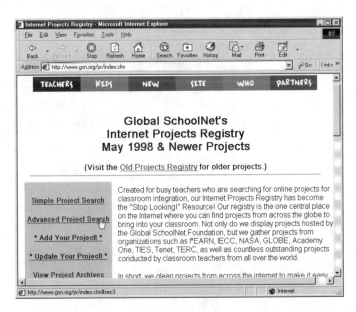

5. Select a *Curriculum* area by clicking in the box.

6. Check the *E-mail* box to select only those projects that will be carried out via e-mail.

7. Click the *Submit Search* button to search the database.

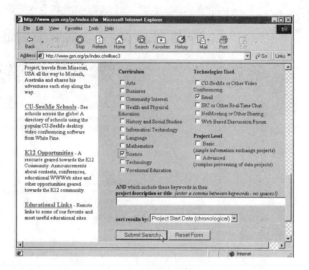

The Projects Registry will return a list of projects to you.

8. Click the hypertext link for each project to read more about it. There will be a contact person's e-mail address listed. You will need to send an e-mail to that person in order to participate.

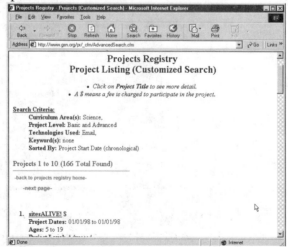

Another Web site that houses online projects is **NickNacks—Telecollaborate**.

They are located at this URL:

http://home.talkcity.com/academydr/nicknacks/

1. Click the *Enter* hyperlink to go to the Web site index page.

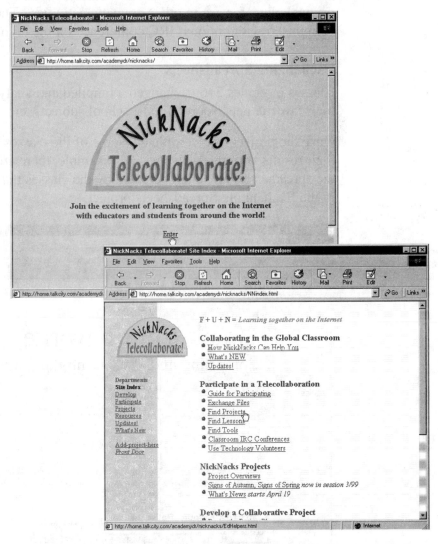

2. You can click the hyperlink *Find Projects* or the hyperlink to read *Examples of Telecollaborations*.

Some projects that have been listed at **NickNacks** include:

Playwriting in the Round

Classes in grades 5–10 collaborated with three classes in the same grade level to write scripts of four mystery plays. Each play consists of four acts, one act written by each of the classes in the script circle. At the conclusion of the project, each class has four original plays for use in other dramatic activities. The activity culminated with optional IRC conference on the dramatic process.

Exchanging Spreadsheets

Classes in grades 2–6 exchanged, compiled and analyzed data on their favorite pets, sports, foods, school subjects, etc.

Once the projects are completed, some of the classes have shared their results with the Web site. For example, there are samples of the spreadsheets and charts created by the classes that participated in the Exchanging Spreadsheets project.

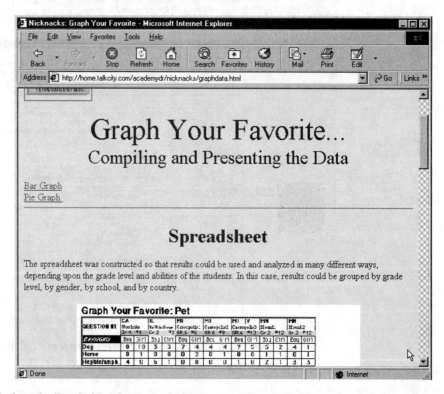

Some Web sites offer you the opportunity to sign up to receive site content and update information. One site that offers this service is **Neuroscience for Kids**. Dr. Eric Chudler at this URL maintains it:

http://weber.u.washington.edu/~chudler/neurok.html

This site has been created for teachers and students and offers information and activities about the nervous system.

1. Scroll down the Table of Contents to see hypertext links to various topics and activities.

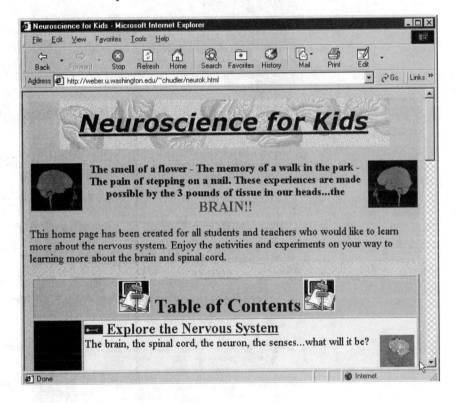

2. Click the *Newsletter* hypertext link.

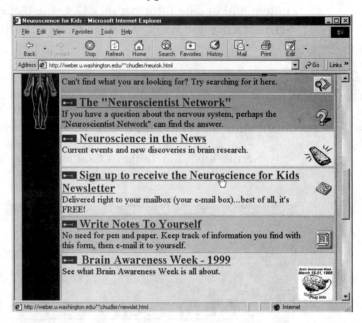

3. To receive the newsletter, click the e-mail hyperlink to send an e-mail message with your e-mail address and a short description of yourself.

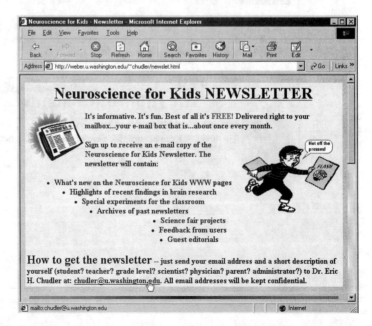

Another Web site which offers a daily e-mail message is **A Word A Day**. You and your students can receive a daily e-mail with a new word and its definition.

It is located at this URL:

http://www.wordsmith.org/awad/

1. Click the hypertext link to *Subscribe* to the newsletter.

2. Fill in your name, e-mail address, and where you heard about **A.W.A.D.**
3. Click the *Subscribe* button.

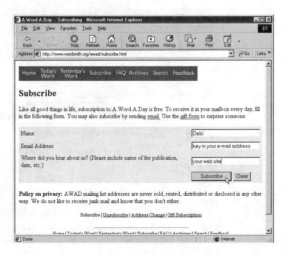

You will receive an e-mail message confirming your subscription. You will then receive an e-mail message each day with a new word, the definition, etymology, a sentence using the word, and links to a sound file with the pronunciation.

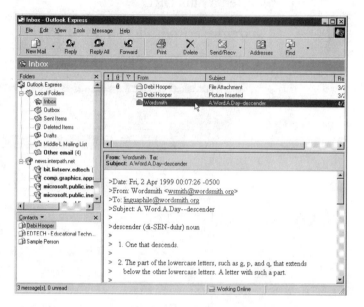

4. Click the hyperlink to hear a pronunciation of the word.

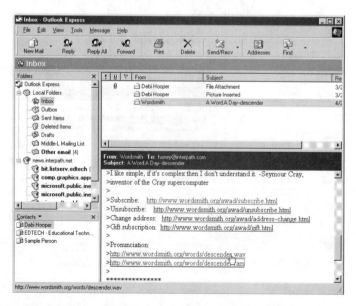

If you do not want to subscribe and receive this in your e-mail every day, you can visit the Web site to see each day's new word.

5. Click the hyperlink to ***Check out Today's Word***.

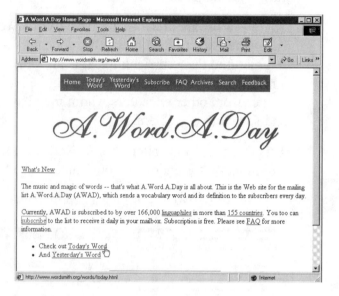

The information about each word is on the Web page.

6. Click the appropriate hyperlink to hear the pronunciation.

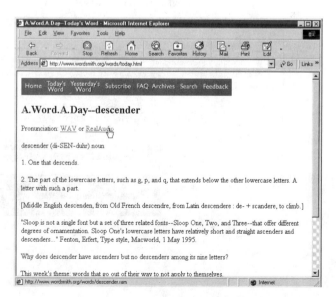

There are also mailing lists to which you can subscribe. You will then receive daily or periodic e-mail messages from other subscribers to the list. Mailing lists or list servers exist for a variety of subjects.

There is a list about using the World Wide Web in education. This is a great place to read how other educators are integrating the Internet into their curriculum. It is also a good forum for posting a message about a problem you might be having and receiving replies from other educators whom may have already encountered and solved that problem.

This mailing list is called **WWWEDU** (pronounced "we do"). Additional information can be found on the Web site at this URL:

http://edweb.gsn.org/wwwedu.html

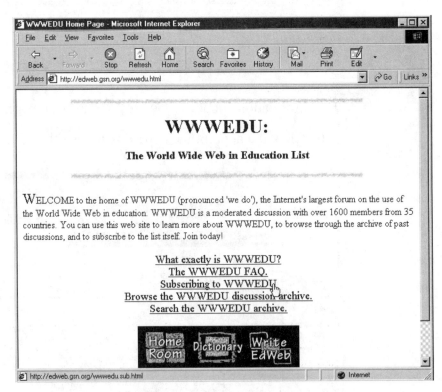

To join **WWWEDU**, you can send a message to

listproc@ready.cpb.org

and in the body of the message, write

subscribe wwwedu your name

and nothing else. You will then be added to the WWWEDU list.
Be sure to put your name where it says 'your name'!

Your e-mail message will look like this:

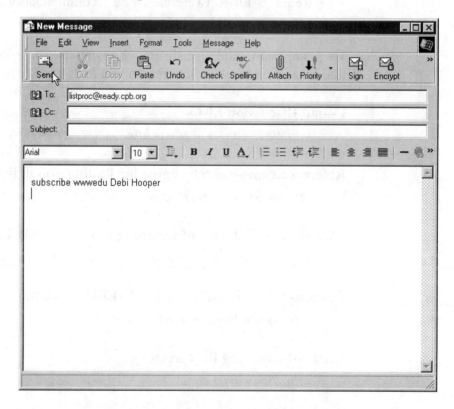

You will receive a welcoming message with information on how
to send messages to the list. When you send in a message, it will
then be sent to all of the members on the list.

When you first join **WWWEDU**, please post an introduction of
yourself to the group, and feel free to suggest any discussion
topics.

Some of the topics discussed on the list have included the following:

- Discussions about new Web sites
- Filtering software
- Notices about conferences
- Calls for authoring articles
- New releases of teaching materials
- Requests for information
- Requests for software/hardware recommendations
- Information about classroom projects

There are many other e-mail lists. You can use these Web sites to find lists about topics of interest to you and your students.

E-mail Discussion Lists

http://edweb.gsn.org/lists.html

Reference.com—search engine for finding e-mail lists

http://www.reference.com/

Blue Web'n—Library of Learning Sites—Weekly Updates

http://www.kn.pacbell.com/wired/bluewebn/

Catalist—the official list of LISTSERV(r) mailing lists

http://www.lsoft.com/lists/listref.html

Liszt—the mailing list directory

http://www.liszt.com/

NeoSoft—Publicly Accessible Mailing Lists

http://www.neosoft.com/internet/paml/

E-mail Discussion Groups

http://www.webcom.com/impulse/list.html

Newsgroups

Outlook Express can also be used to access and participate in newsgroups. Newsgroups are discussion groups about a particular topic or subject. A message sent to a newsgroup is called a "post." A post can be seen by millions of people who choose to read that newsgroup. For Macintosh users, see ***Setting up a Newsgroup Account*** under the ***Help*** menu.

1. You can start setting up your newsgroups by clicking ***Setup a Newsgroup account*** on the *Outlook Express* main page.

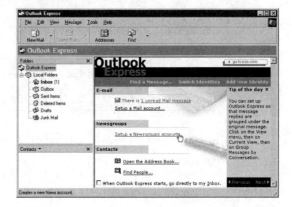

The Internet Connection Wizard will appear.

Some of this information will be the same as your e-mail setup.

2. Make sure your name is correct.
3. Click the ***Next*** button to continue.

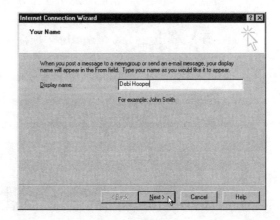

4. Fill in the e-mail address where you want people on the newsgroup to reply.

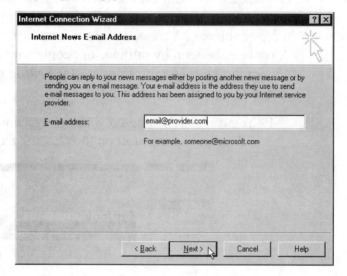

5. Enter the news server name that your Internet Service Provider has given to you.

If you do not have this information, you will need to get it from them.

6. Click the *Next* button to continue.

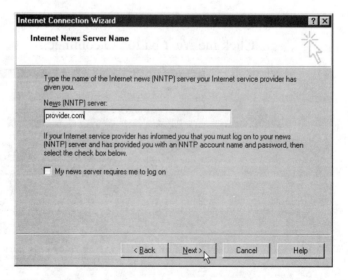

If you have completed all of the steps, you will see the Confirmation dialog box.

7. Click the **Finish** button to return to *Outlook Express* and view the possible newsgroups.

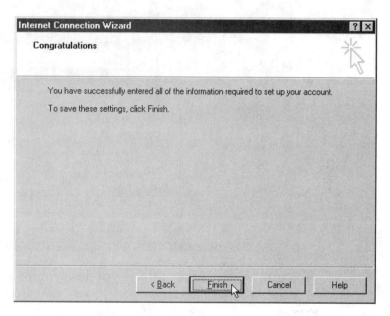

You will then see this dialog box asking if you want to download newsgroups from the new account.

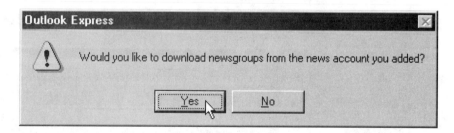

8. Click the *Yes* button to download the list of newsgroup names from your provider.

Note: This may take a few minutes. There are thousands of newsgroups listed. You will only have to download the entire list once.

9. You can subscribe to newsgroups by selecting that option from the *Outlook Express* main screen. This will now appear as an option since you set up your newsgroup account.

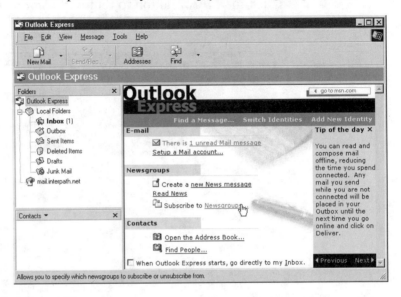

You can browse through the list of newsgroups and select those that are of interest to you.

10. Click the **Subscribe** button to subscribe to a list. For Maintosh users, choose **Subscribe** from the **Tools** menu. You will be able to read the posts without replying to any in order to find out if the list is one in which you want to participate.

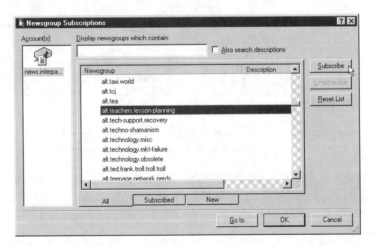

11. You can search the list for a particular key word by entering it in the blank at the top. In this case, you can search for *Internet Explorer* newsgroups by keying in the key word *Internet Explorer*. The newsgroup list will then show all of the possible newsgroups with the word *Explorer* as part of the name. You can then select any that sound like they would fit your needs.

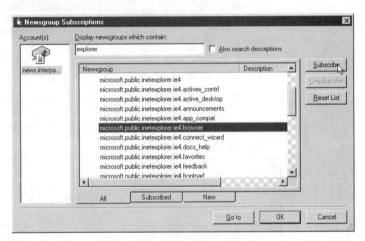

12. Once you have selected one, click the *Subscribe* button to receive that group's posts.

13. If you know the name of the newsgroup you want to subscribe to, key the name into the blank and click the *Subscribe* button.

14. Once you have subscribed to some newsgroups, you can click the newsgroup listing to view the headings.

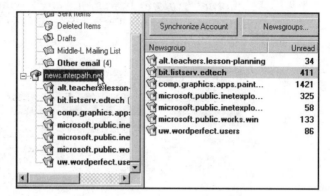

15. You can then double-click a newsgroup header to view the new posts.

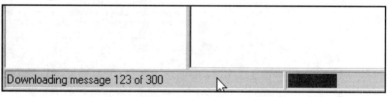

Outlook Express will automatically download up to 300 of the newest posts. This is the default number that is set in the *Options*.

16. You can change that number by choosing *Options* from the *Tools* menu.

17. Select the *Read* tab to edit that setting.

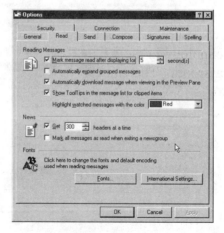

A newsgroup to which you may want to subscribe is the **EDTECH** group. It is offered as a mailing list or as a newsgroup.

You can find information about the **EDTECH** list and newsgroup at this URL:

http://h-net2.msu.edu/~edweb/

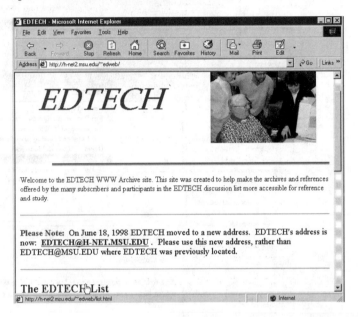

The newsgroup name for the **EDTECH** group is **bit.listserv.edtech**.

The conversations in this newsgroup are about using technology in the classroom. There are discussions about hardware, software, and curriculum.

18. To access the messages in a newsgroup, click that listing.

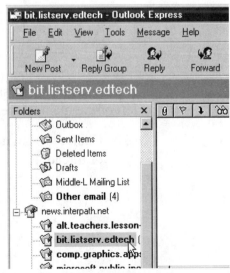

As the messages are downloading, you will see the status at the bottom of the *Outlook Express* window.

The message list will appear in the upper right-hand block of the *Outlook Express* window.

19. Click a message header to read it.

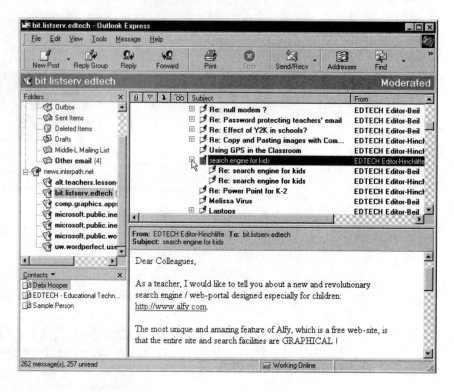

If there are more messages for a topic, there will be a + sign to the left of the main header.

20. Click the + sign to see the rest of the messages for that topic, or thread.

21. If you want to reply to a message, click the ***Reply Group*** button on the tool bar.

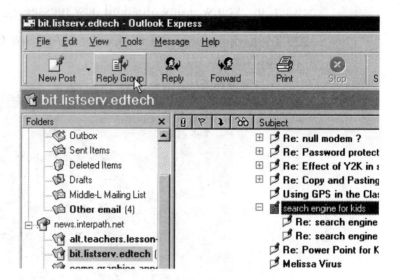

Your reply will go to the newsgroup instead of just to the individual who posted the message.

You will use the Composition utility to type your reply as if you were sending an e-mail message. You should delete part of the original message before sending in order to save space.

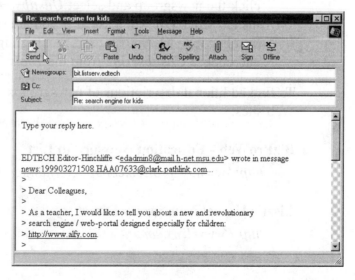

Once you have read the messages you want to read, you can mark the other messages as "read." The next time you access the newsgroup, you will download all new messages.

22. To mark messages as read, select **Mark All Read** from the **Edit** menu.

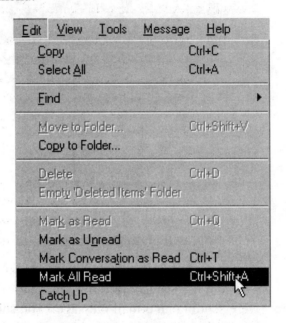

23. To unsubscribe from any of your newsgroups, you can right-click the newsgroup and select **Unsubscribe** from the pop-up menu. Click **OK** when asked if you are sure you want to unsubscribe. Macintosh users can highlight the newsgroup and choose **Unsubscribe** from the **Tools** menu.

To find additional descriptions of newsgroups, you can visit these Web sites.

BizProWeb - Education Newsgroup List

http://www.bizproweb.com/pages/newsgroups/education.html

Liszt's Usenet Newsgroup Directory

http://www.liszt.com/news/

Composing Web Pages

Web pages are created with instructions called HTML or HyperText Markup Language. This programming language was developed so that all computers and browser formats can read it. Whether you have a Windows-based computer or a Macintosh, you will be able to view the same Web pages.

Creating your own Web pages can be one way to improve your school-to-home connection. Parents who have access to the World Wide Web can read your Web pages and find out what is happening in your classroom. Student projects, field trips, on-going class activities, book reviews, and just about any other project can be made into a Web page and shared with other teachers, classes, and parents.

If your school has its own Web server, you can find out how to post your Web pages to it. You will probably need to check with whomever is your "webmaster" or technology person that maintains your network.

If your school does not have its own Web server on-site, there are several Web sites that allow you to have free Web space to publish your own Web pages. These sites make their money from advertisers who pay to have their banner advertisements appear on your Web pages. Some of these sites allow you to pay a monthly fee instead of putting the advertising banners on your page.

Here are some sites with which you can start.

Geocities
http://www.geocities.com

Fortune City
http://www2.fortunecity.com/

Tripod
http://www.tripod.com

Free Sites Network
http://www.fsn.net/

Angelfire
http://www.angelfire.com/

Talk City
http://home.talkcity.com/

Once you visit those sites and decide to start your own Web site, you need to plan what you are going to put in it. Plan carefully. If you design a basic outline of your Web site, you can easily add to it. Otherwise you may wind up with a bunch of Web pages floating up in cyberspace in no particular order.

Here is a brainstorming idea for a classroom Web site.

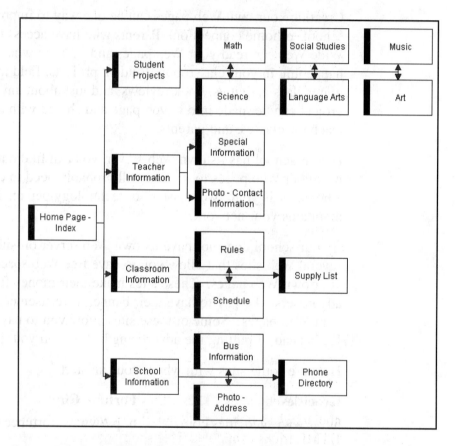

Your home page should be an index to the rest of the Web site. You can direct visitors to the main headings and then include more specific ideas within those groupings.

If you would like more detailed information about planning a Web site and HTML programming, check out a book from Teacher Created Materials, *A Beginner's Guide to Creating Web Pages for School or Classroom.*

Before creating any Web pages, you should set up a folder on your hard drive in which to keep your Web pages and any other files organized. You may just want to name this folder Webpages. Your entire HTML files, graphics, or multimedia files should be saved to this folder.

Note: *FrontPage Express* is currently not available for the Macintosh. You may want to purchase the full version of *FrontPage* for the Macintosh.

To create Web pages, you need to start the *FrontPage Express* program.

To do this double-click the icon or a shortcut icon.

You can also choose to edit a Web page you are viewing in *Internet Explorer*.

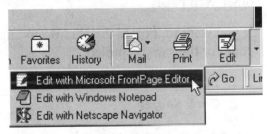

To show how *FrontPage Express* works, you will be looking at sample Web pages. These illustrate how you can post information about a class field trip. You will see samples of just a few of the HTML tricks available. This should give you a starting point for creating simple Web pages of your own.

To follow along with the instructions, select the *Sample Field Trip* Web pages from the CD-ROM that accompanies this book.

This set of sample Web pages represents a school field trip to Washington, D.C. There are photographs and captions throughout the pages. Each of the pages has HTML applications that you can use.

The first process before starting a Web page project is to set up a plan. This is the basic plan for the Field Trip Web pages.

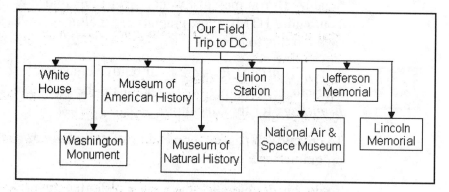

An actual field trip to Washington, D.C. would certainly have more headings for places visited, but this is a simple project to give you some ideas about what you can do. As long as you have space enough to hold your files, you can always add more.

The introductory page has a heading, a graphic, and links to the other Web pages.

If you want to look at the HTML coding, you can view the source code for the sample project.

1. In *Internet Explorer*, click *View*.
2. Click *Source*.

You will see a separate window open with text instructions in it. Look at the middle section to get an idea of the instructions that make this page look the way that it does.

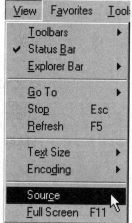

The body of the page has instructions like this:

<body bgcolor="#FFFFFF">

<h1 align="center">Our Class Field Trip</h1>

<h1 align="center">To Washington, D.C.</h1>

<p> </p>

<p align="center"><img src="file:///E:/IEBook/WEBPAGE/Dc508.jpg" alt="Morning Glories" width="400" height="274"></p>

<p align="left">We visited many of the museums and landmarks in our nation's capital.

Click the links below to see some of our photos. </p>

<p align="left"><a href="white.htm">White House</a>

<a href="wash-mon.htm">Washington Monument</a>

<a href="am-hist.htm">Museum of American History</a>

<a href="nat-hist.htm">Museum of Natural History</a>

<a href="union.htm">Union Station</a>

<a href="air-space.htm">National Air & Space Museum</a>

<a href="jefferson.htm">Jefferson Memorial</a>

<a href="lincoln.htm">Lincoln Memorial</a>

</p>

</body>

</html>

There are two heading lines at the top of the page.

There is a graphic of flowers.

Then there is text followed by a list of hypertext links to the other pages.

This is a very simple Web page. *FrontPage Express* writes all of these instructions for you as you select various options. Here is how that page was created.

Creating a Centered Heading

1. Key in the text for your heading.

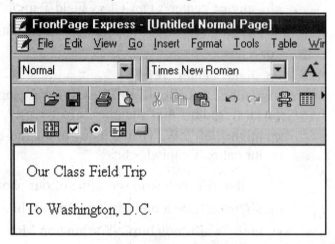

2. Use your mouse to highlight or block the text.

3. Click the drop-down menu that says **Normal**.

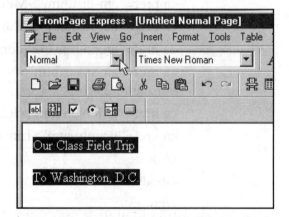

4. Select **Heading 1** from the drop-down menu choices.

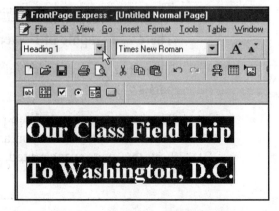

5. Click *Format*.

6. Select *Paragraph*.

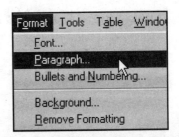

You can use this option to set the *Heading* format.

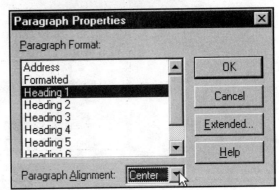

7. Select *Center* from the *Paragraph Alignment* choices.

8. You can also click the centering alignment button on the toolbar.

Your heading is now centered at the top of the window.

Inserting a Graphic Image

1. Click the *Insert Image* button on the tool bar.

2. Click the *Browse* button on the *Image* dialog box to find the file you want to insert.

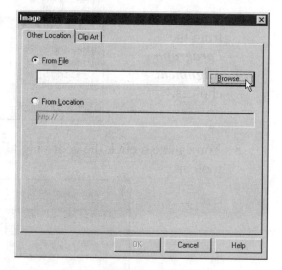

3. Select the image file from your Web page folder.

Note: You should have put all of your graphics in this folder before starting to create the Web pages.

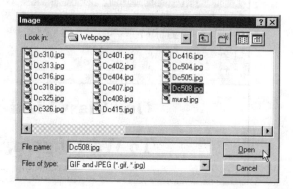

The image will automatically appear in your Web page.

4. To edit the properties of that file, right-click the image.

5. Then select *Image Properties* from the pop-up menu.

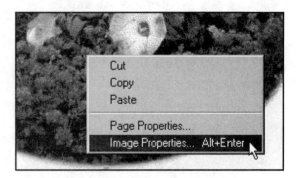

Some browser software will not view graphics, and some people have slow Internet connection speeds so they turn off graphic viewing. By inserting a text description of each image, you are providing those Internet users with an idea of what each image is.

6. Enter a simple description of the image in the *Text:* blank.

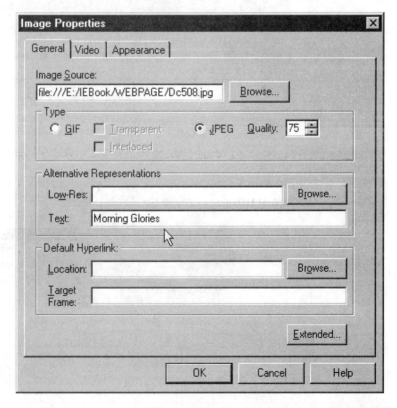

7. To make sure your graphic retains its size, select the **Appearance** tab.

8. Click the **Specify Size** blank.

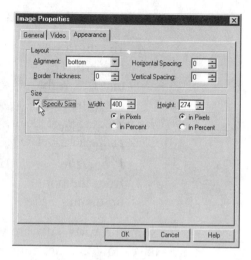

You will then have the option of designating a width and height in pixels or choosing a percentage of the Web page space.

Your graphic image is now located just under the heading. If it is aligned to the left, you can click to select it and center it in the same way you centered the heading.

The rest of this page is keyed in as plain text. Press **Shift/Enter** to single space the text in the list. Once the list is keyed in, it can then be set up as hypertext links.

Creating a Hypertext Link

1. Use your mouse to highlight or block the text that will become a hyperlink .

2. Click the *Create or Edit Hyperlink* button on the tool bar.

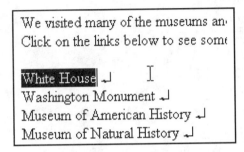
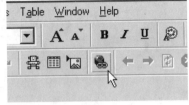

If you want the hyperlink to refer to a Web page already on the World Wide Web, key in that URL on the *World Wide Web* tab.

3. In this case, we want to link to a new page. Click the *New Page* tab.

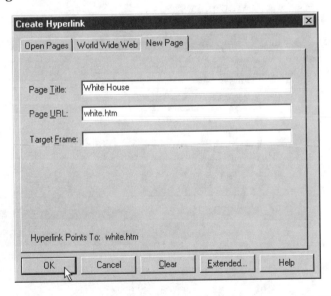

FrontPage Express has already assumed that you want to name the new page *white.htm*.

4. If this is correct, click the *OK* button to continue. Otherwise, key in the file name you want to use.

FrontPage Express wants to know what kind of Web page you will be creating.

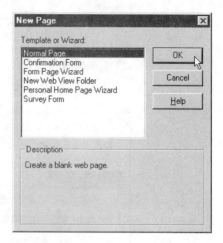

5. Select the *Normal Page* setting. You will be creating this page at a later time.

6. A new blank Web page is automatically created. To work on it at a later time, select *Save* from the *File* menu.

7. Click the *As File* button to save this as a file rather than publishing it to a Web site.

8. Save the Web page in the folder with your graphics and other Web pages.

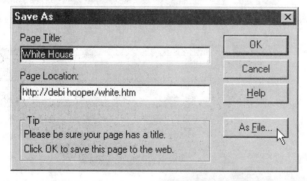

9. To return to your original Web page, select it from the *Window* drop-down menu.

10. You can also choose *Close* from the *File* menu to close the new, blank Web page.

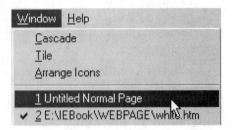

11. Continue to create hyperlinks for all of the other titles in your list. The hypertext links will appear in a different color text (blue) and will be underlined. This is the default setting for Web pages. You can change this later if you choose.

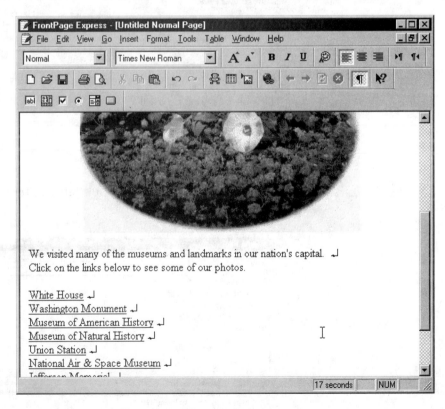

Saving Your Web Page

You should save your Web page often while you are working on it.

1. Click the *Save* button on the tool bar.

2. Make sure your page has a title. *FrontPage Express* may choose the beginning text on the page to be the title, but you can change that if necessary.

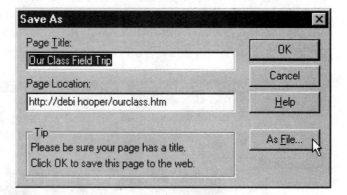

3. Click the *As File* button to save this page as a file in your folder.

4. Give the page a file name and click *Save* in the *Save As File* dialog box.

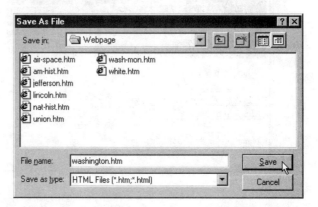

As you browse through the sample Web pages on the CD-ROM, you will see more techniques. These are all simple techniques that you can easily do on your own pages.

The **White House** and **Washington Monument** Web pages are very simple. There is a heading, a graphic image, and a hypertext link back to the main index page. You should always provide visitors to your pages with a way back to the main page.

The **Museum of American History** Web page has more graphic images and more text. The images are not centered as on the first pages. You will also see a hypertext link at the bottom of the Web page that allows visitors to return to the index page.

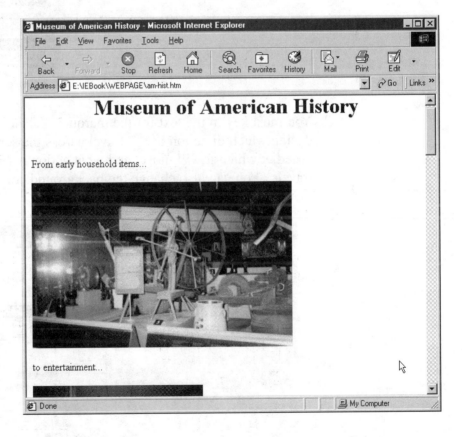

Inserting a Marquee

The Web page for the **Museum of Natural History** uses a different technique for providing captions. When inserting a marquee, you can decide to have the text enter the Web page in a variety of ways. This web page shows you several different marquee formats.

1. To insert a marquee, select *Marquee* from the *Insert* drop-down menu.

2. You must key in the text for the marquee. Then you can decide which direction it will travel across the screen, the speed at which it will move, and what action it will take as it travels. You can also change the background color of the marquee itself.

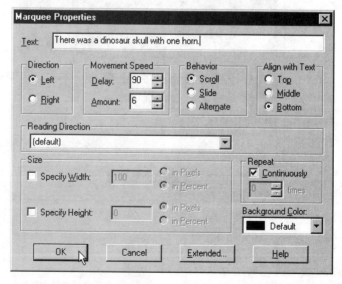

Note: You would not want to use this option as much as it is used on this Web page. This is just a sample of the variety of marquee signs.

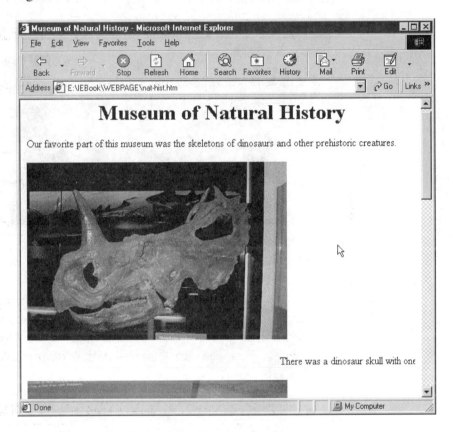

3. Click your **Refresh** button several times as you view the different marquee styles on this Web page.

Image Hyperlink

The **Union Station** Web page uses a small graphic image near the bottom of the Web page as a hyperlink to a larger image.

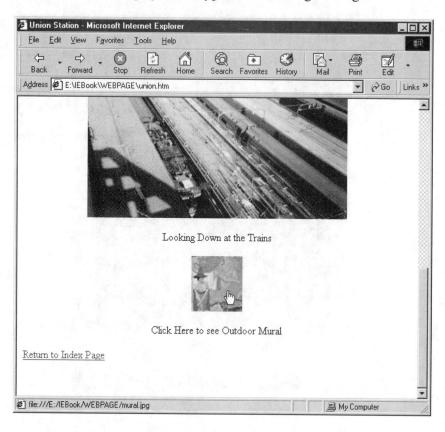

1. In *FrontPage Express*, select the image that will be used as the hyperlink.

2. Click the ***Create or Edit Hyperlink*** button on the tool bar.

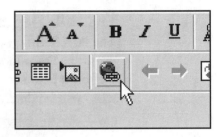

3. Enter the Web page URL or a link to another image file in the ***URL:*** blank of the ***Edit Hyperlink*** dialog box.

This link takes the user to a graphic image.

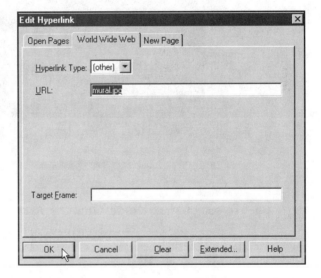

If the link takes users to another graphic image, you should make sure they know how to click the ***Back*** button of their browser to return to the original Web page.

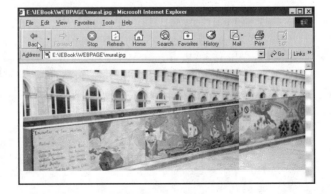

Page and Text Color

The **Air & Space Museum** page adds three more processes. It uses a background color and a text color other than black and white. It also uses a table to organize the graphic images. The table will be discussed in the next section.

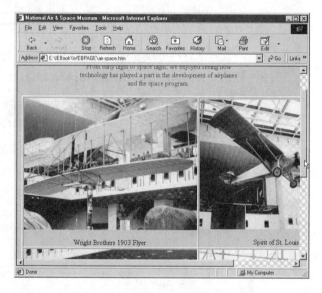

1. To select a text color, click the *Text Color* button.

2. Once you see the color palette, select the text color of your choice. You can also click the *Define Custom Colors* button and customize your own color.

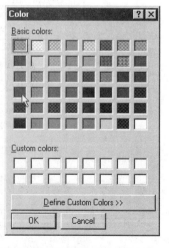

3. To change the background color of the Web page, select **Background** from the **Format** drop-down menu.

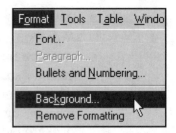

4. Select a color from the **Background** menu.
5. You can also click **Custom** at the bottom of the list and select another color.

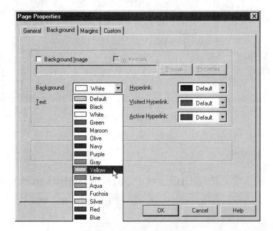

6. If you select **Custom**, you will be able to choose from the entire palette of colors.

7. Click the **OK** button to return to your Web page.

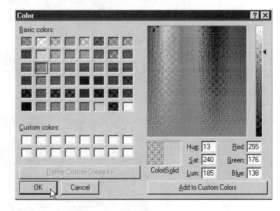

Note: If you use a background image, it will override the color choice. It is still a good idea to use a complementary background color for those users who do not load images.

Tables

You should be sure to plan ahead before you create a table to organize images or information. You will need to know how many cells, or spaces, to include in your table. You should also decide whether you want the table background to be the same as the Web page background, or if you would rather have a different color or a background image.

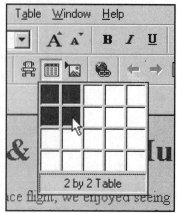

1. Click the *Table* button and move your cursor to select the width and height of your table. For this page, there are two rows and two columns.

2. Position your cursor within the table cell, and enter any information or images you want.

Wright Brothers 1903 Flyer

3. To edit any of the table formatting, select **Table Properties** from the **Table** drop-down menu.

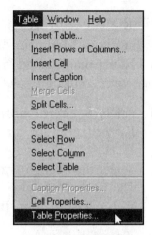

4. For example, if you want a border around each of your table cells, you can select a border size from the **Table Properties** dialog box.

5. You can also select different background and border colors at this point.

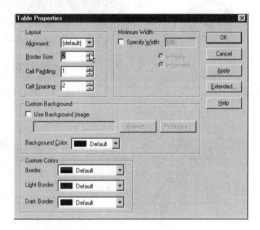

You can use a table on your classroom Web site as a way of posting your classroom schedule.

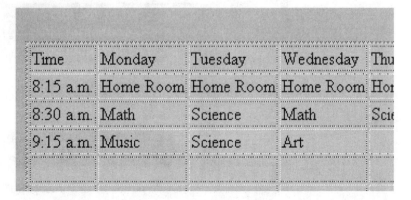

Background Images

The **Jefferson Memorial** Web page has a background image. It is a border image with color on the left side.

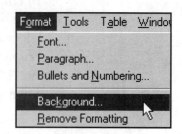

1. Select ***Background*** from the ***Format*** drop-down menu.

2. Select the background image you wish to use on the page. The background image should be in the same folder as the Web page and any other graphics.

Note: Some Web page providers will only handle GIF files as background images. Read their information if you are unable to view your background image after uploading it to a Web site.

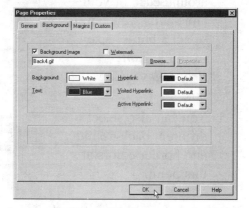

3. Click the ***OK*** button to apply the formatting to the Web page.

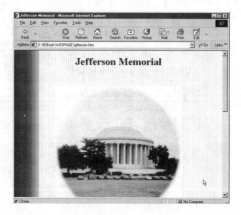

Scrolling Text Box

The **Lincoln Memorial** Web page uses a scrolling text box technique. This is useful if you have a large quantity of text that you want to have appear in a concise area on the Web page.

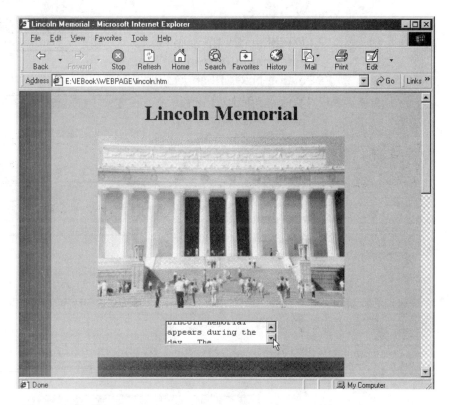

On this page, the paragraphs of text appear in a very small box beneath the photographs. Visitors to the Web page can use the arrows to scroll down to read the rest of each paragraph.

1. To create the text box, click the ***Scrolling Text Box*** button on the tool bar.

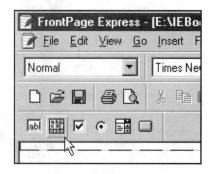

The text box tool will appear in the *FrontPage Express* window.

It is a representation of a text box and will not appear this small in your Web page.

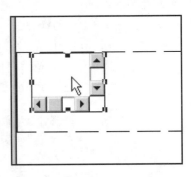

2. Double-click the graphic to enter or edit text in the box. A dialog box will appear.

3. You can leave the name of the text box as it appears. Enter the text in the *Initial value:* blank.

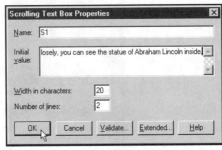

4. Set the width of the box and the number of lines you want to appear on the Web page.

5. Click the *OK* button to continue.

6. To center the text box, click the graphic and center it on the Web page.

The text box will be a small graphic in the *FrontPage Express* window but will appear in the size you set on the actual Web page.

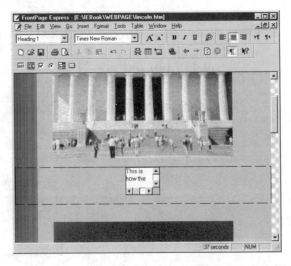

Creating a New Web Page

When you complete one Web page and are ready to start a new page, you can click the *New* button on *FrontPage Express*'s tool bar.

Clicking the *New* button will start a blank normal Web page. You can then start creating your own design.

If you need some help getting started with designing your Web pages, you can use the "Wizards" which are available. These are program utilities that guide you through creating a Web page.

1. Select *New* from the *File* menu.

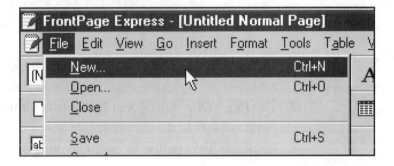

2. You will be able to select from several types of Wizards. For this example, we have selected the *Personal Home Page Wizard*.

3. Click the *OK* button to continue.

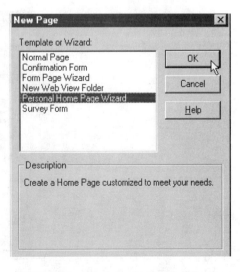

4. Your first choice will be to select the major sections in your new Web page.

5. Click the *Next* button to continue.

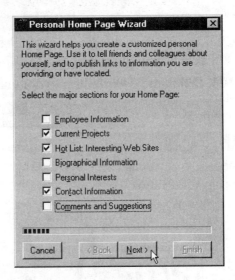

6. The wizard then asks for a *Page URL*. Enter a Web page name.

7. The *Page Title* will appear as the title on the Web page. Enter a name here.

8. Click the *Next* button to continue creating your Web page.

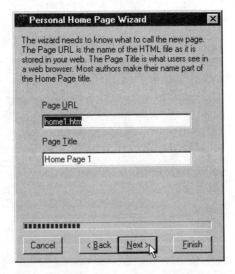

The Wizard will then ask you questions based on the major sections you chose to have in your Web page.

9. You will select titles for the ***Current Projects***.

10. You can also select how you want them to appear in the Web page. They can be a simple list or a list with an explanation or definition.

11. Click the ***Next*** button to continue.

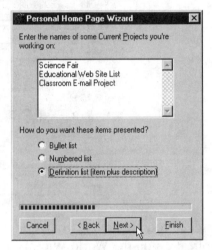

12. You are then asked to ***Choose the Presentation style for your Hot List of Interesting Web Sites***.

13. Click the ***Next*** button to continue.

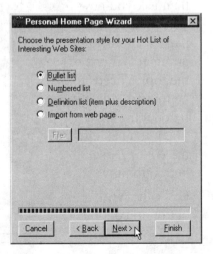

14. If you choose to have **Contact Information** on your Web page, you will be asked to enter various types of information.

15. Click the **Next** button to continue.

Note: If you are having your students create Web pages for publication on the World Wide Web, be sure to caution them against entering personal data such as address and phone numbers on a Web page.

16. The Wizard will then ask you how you want your Web page sections to be arranged. If one of the topics needs to be moved, select it by clicking it. Then you can click the **Up** or **Down** button to move it.

17. Click the **Next** button to continue.

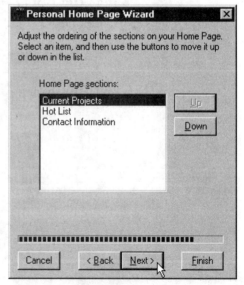

18. Congratulations! Once you have finished answering all of the questions, you can click the *Finish* button and wait while the Wizard formats your Web page.

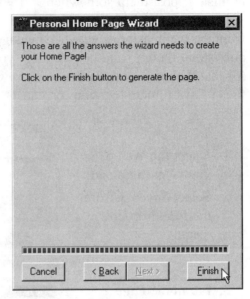

19. This Web page is a template for you to edit. You can now highlight different areas of text and replace them with your own specific information.

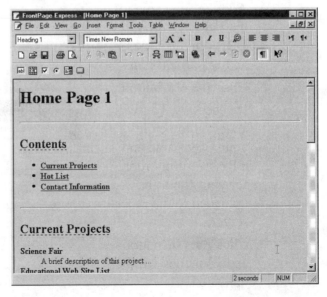

Publishing Web Pages

Once you have finished creating your Web pages, you will want to publish or post them somewhere. If you are publishing them to your school's Web site, you will need to get specific directions from the webmaster or network manager at school. If you are publishing them to another location, you can enter the information for that Web site and *FrontPage Express* will upload (move) your files to that remote location for you.

1. Select the Web page you want to upload.

2. Select **Save As** from the **File** drop-down menu.

3. Fill in the **Page Location**. You will get this information from the web site provider.

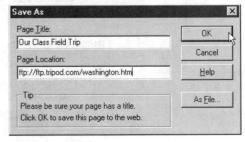

4. Add the file name to the **Page Location** URL. In this case, add *washington.htm*.

5. Click the **OK** button.

6. If necessary, you will be asked to key in your User name and a Password in order for your file to be uploaded to the other server.

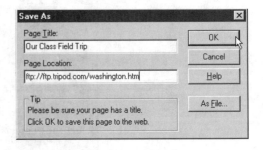

7. Click the **OK** button and your files will be uploaded.

Meeting in Cyber Space

Another utility that accompanies the *Internet Explorer* software is *NetMeeting*. It will allow you to set up meetings with people all over the world but they will need to have the software installed on their computer as well. Then you can chat, talk via microphone, share files, browse the Web together, and view graphics on the Whiteboard.

Note: *NetMeeting* is not available for the Macintosh.

To start *NetMeeting*, double-click the icon or its shortcut.

You will see this splash screen as *NetMeeting* is starting.

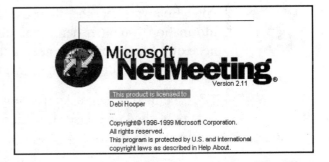

Setting Up *NetMeeting*

The first time you use *NetMeeting*, you will see this screen. This is the beginning of the Wizard that will help you set up your computer.

1. Click the *Next* button to continue.

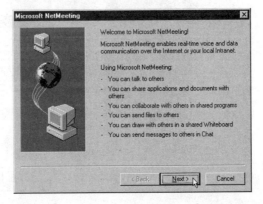

2. Fill in your name and e-mail address so that other users can contact you.

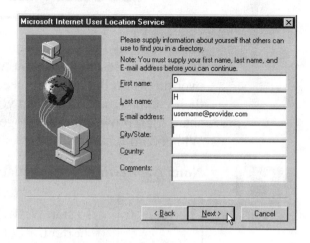

If your students will be using this, you may decide to simply use a classroom or school name.

Note: Be aware that the other users will be able to read all of the information you enter here. You do not have to include every piece of information. You need only to enter an e-mail address in order to have other users "call" you on this software.

3. The next screen asks if you want to have your name published on a User Location Server so that other users can contact you.

Note: Again, if you are using this in your classroom, you may decide not to be on a contact list. Other users can contact you via your e-mail address. You do not have to be listed on a general list.

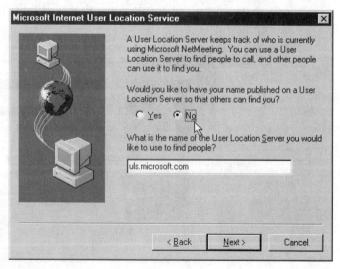

If you have a microphone and speakers hooked up to your computer, the Wizard can help you with your audio settings.

4. Close any other programs that use sound.

5. Click the *Next* button.

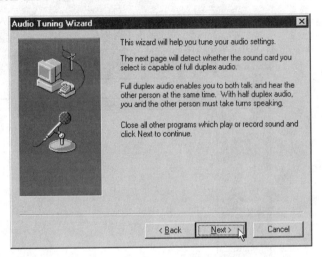

6. Continue through the audio tests.

7. Select your modem speed when you are prompted by the Wizard.

8. Click the *Next* button.

The Wizard will let you know when *NetMeeting* is completely set up.

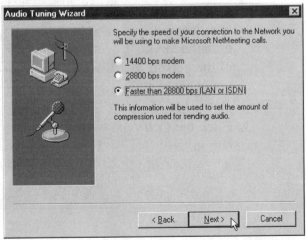

Contacting Other Users

Once you have *NetMeeting* set up, you can contact other users.

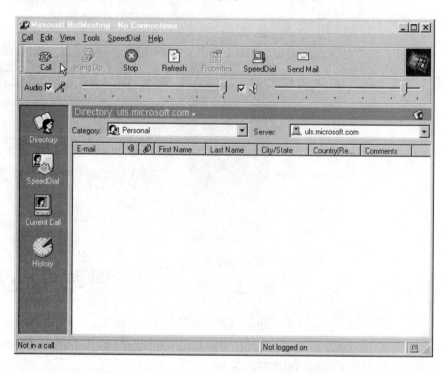

1. If you know their e-mail addresses, you can click the *Call* button to contact them.

2. In the *New Call* dialog box, key in the e-mail address of the person you want to call.

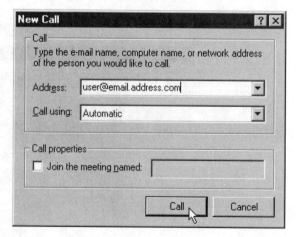

3. Click the *Call* button.

If the person you are trying to contact is not online or the e-mail address you keyed in is incorrect, *NetMeeting* will reply with an error message letting you know that the person could not be located.

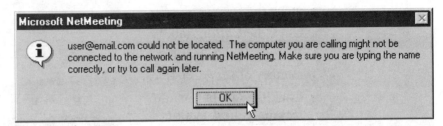

There may also be a problem with your connection to a *NetMeeting* network.

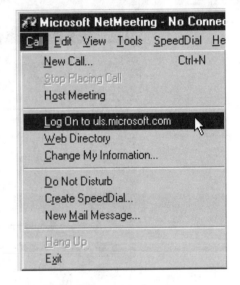

4. Select the **Log On** option on the **Call** menu to make sure you are logged onto a network.

If that network is busy, *NetMeeting* will reply with an error message. You will be advised to change the server selection.

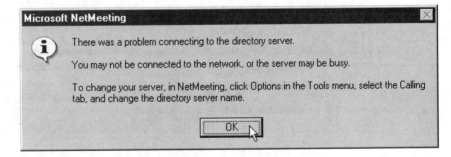

5. In order to select a different *NetMeeting* network, click **Options** on the *Tools* drop-down menu.

6. Click the **Calling** tab.

7. You can then select from a number of server choices.

8. Click the **OK** button after making your selection.

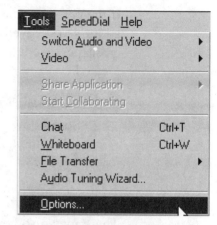

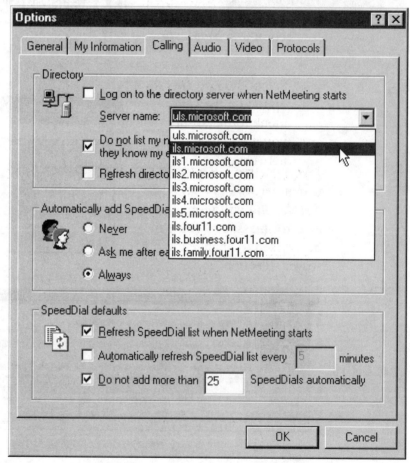

When you are connected, you can view a list of other people who are logged on to the same network.

1. Click the *Directory* bar.
2. Scroll down the list and select the network you want to view.

You will most likely not want your students to be doing this unless they are being closely supervised.

3. *NetMeeting* will show you a list of all of the users logged into that network. You can contact any users by double-clicking this listing. They can then respond if they want to reply to you.

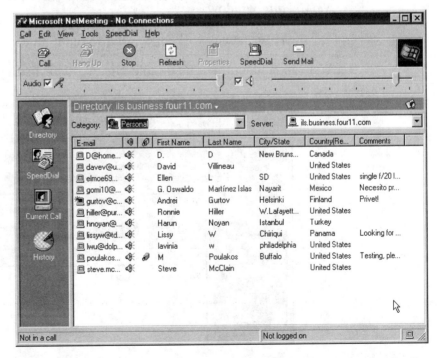

If there are other users (teachers, classrooms) you will be contacting often, you can set up a *SpeedDial* option.

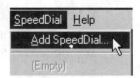

1. Select *Add SpeedDial* from the *SpeedDial* menu.

2. Enter a user's e-mail address and select *Add to SpeedDial list*.

3. Click the OK button to add that user to your list.

Once you have users set up in your *SpeedDial*, you can access them by clicking the *SpeedDial* button on the left-hand side of the *NetMeeting* window.

A list of user names will appear on the right.

You can contact them by double-clicking their listing.

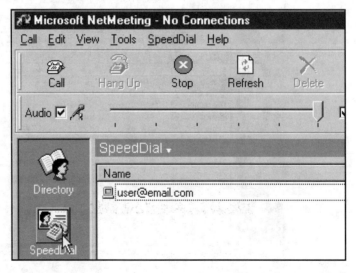

File Sharing

You can choose to send files to another user through the *File Transfer* utility.

1. Once you are connected to other user(s), select the *File Transfer* option from the *Tools* drop-down menu.

2. Click *Send File*.

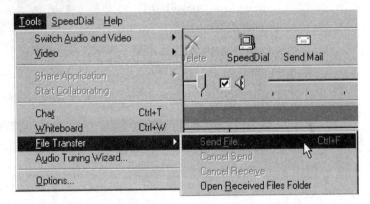

3. Browse through the list of your files until you find the correct one.

4. Once you select the file, you will be sending it to all of the users you are connected to at that time.

5. In order to view files sent to you by other users, you would click *Tools* and select *File Transfer*.

6. Select *Open Received Files Folder*. Once that folder is open, you can view those files in their corresponding programs.

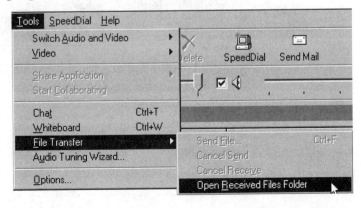

Using the Whiteboard

The *Whiteboard* is a drawing tool that allows you to share a diagram or drawing with the other user(s) connected to you.

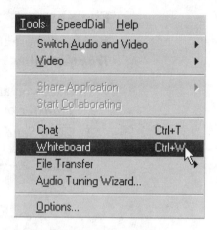

1. To open the *Whiteboard*, select *Whiteboard* from the *Tools* drop-down menu.

This will open a drawing board much like the simple draw programs that come as part of your normal operating system.

2. Copy and paste other diagrams into position in the drawing window and use the tools to write, draw, or point out certain parts of the diagram.

There is a shortcut button for copying and pasting diagrams or images into the *Whiteboard* window.

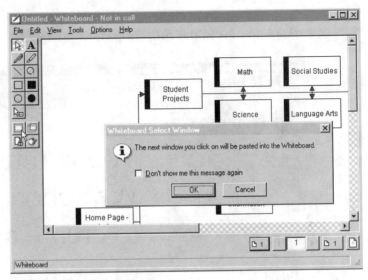

3. Click the *Select Window* button on the tool bar and the next window you click will be pasted into the *Whiteboard* blank.

The *Whiteboard* also has a pointer in the shape of a hand that you can move around a diagram or image while discussing it with other users.

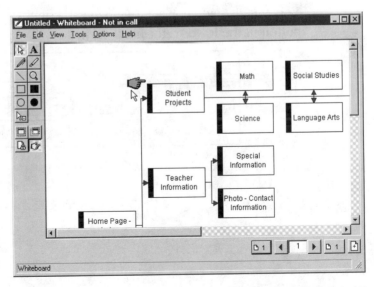

The ***Whiteboard*** can also be used to create a simple slide show presentation to share with other users.

To insert additional pages into your slide show, use the ***Insert Page*** options in the ***Edit*** drop-down menu.

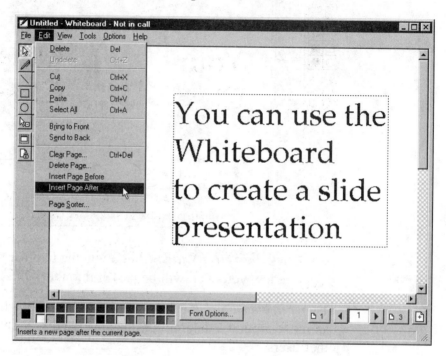

You can also add consecutive pages by clicking the ***Add Page*** button in the lower right-hand corner.

Your class and another class can collaborate on projects through the *Whiteboard* slide show option.

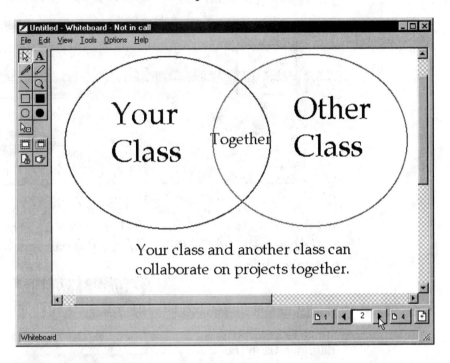

Each class can be responsible for separate parts of the slide show. The pages can then be added together and organized.

To organize slides within the slide show, select *Page Sorter* from the *Edit* drop-down menu.

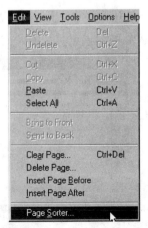

The *Page Sorter* utility allows you to move slides into the order in which they will appear in the slide show.

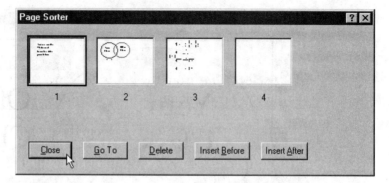

You can use this utility to view all of the slides in the slide show and then quickly go to a specific slide to edit it. First select the slide, then click the *Go To* button. Or you can double-click that particular slide.

You and your students can save slide shows or diagrams from the *Whiteboard* by selecting *Save* from the *File* drop-down menu.

The file will be saved as a *WHT* format file. This can then be sent to anyone with *NetMeeting* to open and view.

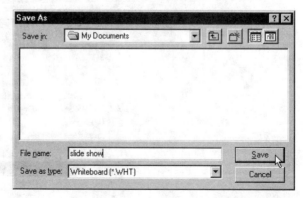

Chatting via *NetMeeting*

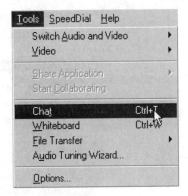

You can chat in *NetMeeting* by typing as well as by using a microphone.

1. To use the **Chat** option, select *Chat* from the *Tools* drop-down menu.

2. Type your message in the *Message:* blank.
3. Press the *Enter* key or click the *Send* button to post the message to all of the users.

You can also select a specific user from the *Send To:* list.

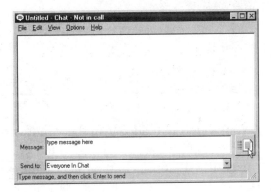

Once you send the message, it will appear in the chat box along with messages from other users.

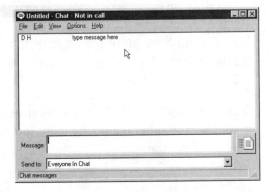

If you have a digital video camera connected to your computer, you can share live video via *NetMeeting*.

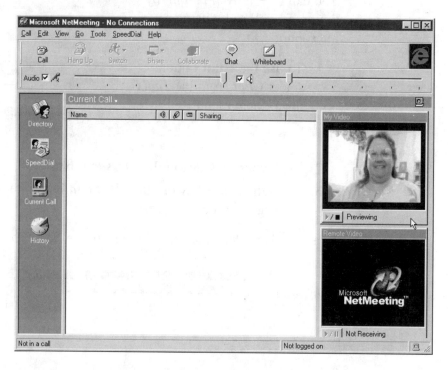

Your video will appear in the window on the main *NetMeeting* screen. If you are receiving video transmission from the other user, it will appear in the lower window.

With a good Internet connection, you can easily transmit both audio and video. In this way, you can talk "live" to people anywhere in the world.

Each of *NetMeeting*'s utilities is designed for a different purpose, but you can have more than one utility open at a time. You can be transmitting video while you are chatting and working on the **Whiteboard**.

You can use this ability to share entire classroom activities with students at another school or even in another classroom within your own school.

Select the ***Detach*** options from the ***View*** drop-down menu to move the video screens around on your desktop.

You can then position several of *NetMeeting*'s utilities on your screen at one time.

Finding Answers to Your Questions

There are several ways to find answers to questions you may have about using Microsoft *Internet Explorer* and all of its components.

The first place you should look is the official **Microsoft** Web site. There is information about *Internet Explorer* version 5.x as well as a download center for downloading upgrades and plug-ins. Support information is also available.

The URL for the *Internet Explorer* 5 Web site is:

> *http://www.microsoft.com/windows/ie/*

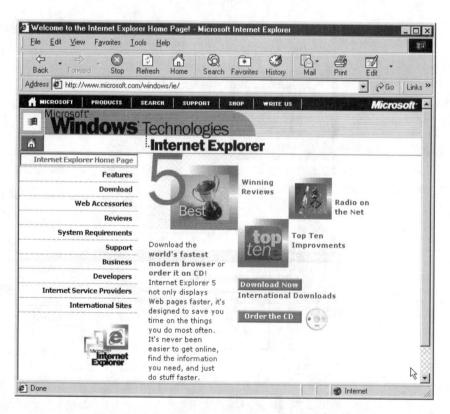

Another way to find answers is to ask someone. There are several newsgroups to which you can subscribe that will provide answers to a variety of *Internet Explorer* questions. The newsproups are in the group:

msnews.microsoft.com.

You may have to add a new newsgroup account in order to view these newsgroups.

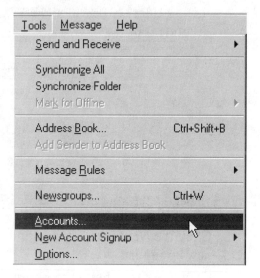

1. Select **Accounts** from the **Tools** drop-down menu.
2. Click the **Add** button and select **News**.

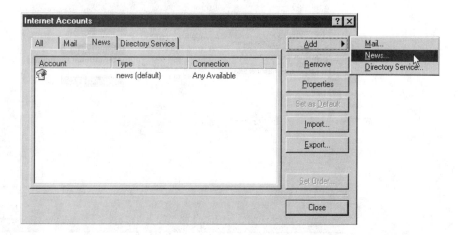

3. Follow the screen instructions and enter your name and e-mail address. Click the *Next* button until you reach this screen.

4. Key in the group name: *msnews.microsoft.com*

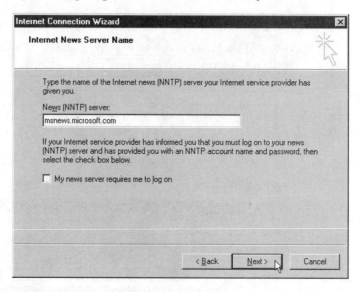

5. Click the *Next* button to continue adding this group to your newsgroup list.

6. Click the *Close* button to return to *Outlook Express*.

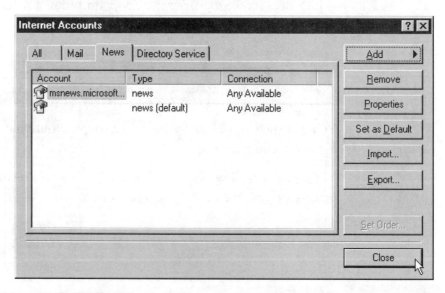

Outlook Express will ask if you want to download the newsgroups from this new account.

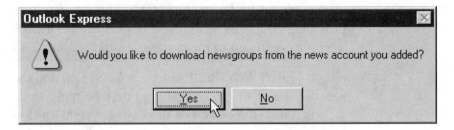

7. Click the **Yes** button to download the list of available newsgroups.

8. Search for newsgroups about *Internet Explorer* 5 by keying in *ie5* in the search window.

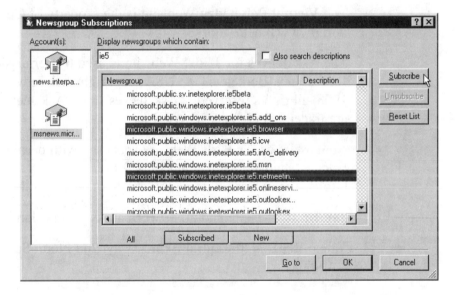

You can then subscribe to the newsgroups about your *Internet Explorer* components.

Refer to the **Newsgroups** section (page 253) to find out how to receive and answer newsgroup messages.

Copyright Credits

Web sites referred to in this book have been used with permission of the creators and/or webmasters. Thanks go to these sites for providing educators with resources for use in their classrooms. Specific credits go to these sites:

Excite Search Web site: *Excite*, *Excite* Search and the *Excite* Logo are trademarks of *Excite*, Inc. and may be registered in various jurisdictions. *Excite* screen display copyright 1995–1999 *Excite*, Inc.

Special thanks to the contributors to **MidLink Magazine**. Schools and students from around the world provide all of these projects and activities.

The **Virtual Polyhedra** Web site is the property of George Hart, http://www.li.net/~george.

The **Ask Jeeves for Kids!** Web site is used by permission of Ask Jeeves, Inc., Berkeley, CA, USA, copyright Ask Jeeves, Inc. 1997-1998, all rights reserved. "Ask Jeeves" and "Ask Jeeves for Kids" are trademarks of Ask Jeeves, Inc.

Neuroscience for Kids Web site was used with permission of Dr. Eric H. Chudler, Neuroscience for Kids, http://weber.u.washington.edu/~chudler/neurok.html.

Jan Brett Web site and all artwork are copyright Jan Brett.

Yahoo! Inc., 3420 Central Expressway, 2nd Floor, Santa Clara, CA 95051

Glossary

Bookmark—A way to store a Web address (URL) without having to write it down to remember it.

Browser—The program that allows you to access and read hypertext documents on the network or on the World Wide Web.

Cache—An area in memory or on your hard disk where copies of frequently accessed web pages and graphics are stored for quick retrieval.

Download—To save a file or web page from the Internet or a network file server to your computer's hard disk or a floppy disk.

E-mail—(Electronic Mail) A system for sending and receiving text messages and attached files between locations via the computer.

FAQ—(Frequently Asked Questions) A Web page found at many Web sites which provides answers to most questions you may have about that web site.

Favorite—see Bookmark

Frame—A divided section of a Web page.

History—A stored list of Web sites visited by your computer. This list is kept for a specified number of days.

HTML—HyperText Markup Language—The coding language used to create hypertext documents for use on the World Wide Web.

HTTP—HyperText Transfer Protocol—The process for moving hypertext files across the Internet.

Internet—The collection of over 60,000 inter-connected networks.

Mailing list—A list to which you can send e-mail that will automatically be forwarded to all members of the list group.

Glossary *(cont.)*

Newsgroup—A discussion group about a particular topic or subject.

Scrolling—Using your mouse or arrow keys to navigate up and down a Web page.

Search engine—A Web site which offers searching capabilities for you to find links to various Web sites that meet your search criteria.

Subscribe—Signing up for a mailing list or newsgroup.

Template—A sample Web page that you can edit to easily create your own Web page.

Thread—All the messages in a mailing list or newsgroup which follow a specific topic.

URL—(Uniform Resource Locator) The Internet address of a Web page.

Index

Index *(cont.)*